RUSSIAN CIVIL WAR

RED TERROR, WHITE TERROR
1917–1922

MICHAEL FOLEY

Pen & Sword
MILITARY

To Gary and Maureen, old friends are the best friends

First published in Great Britain in 2018 by
PEN AND SWORD MILITARY
an imprint of
Pen and Sword Books Ltd
47 Church Street
Barnsley
South Yorkshire S70 2AS

Copyright © Michael Foley, 2018

ISBN 978 1 526728 61 6

The right of Michael Foley to be identified as the author of this work
has been asserted in accordance with the Copyright, Designs and Patents Act 1988.

Typeset by Aura Technology and Software Services, India
Printed and bound by CPI Group (UK) Ltd, Croydon, CR0 4YY

Pen & Sword Books Ltd incorporates the imprints of Pen & Sword
Archaeology, Atlas, Aviation, Battleground, Discovery, Family History, History, Maritime, Military,
Naval, Politics, Railways, Select, Social History, Transport, True Crime, Claymore Press, Frontline Books,
Leo Cooper, Praetorian Press, Remember When, Seaforth Publishing and Wharncliffe.

For a complete list of Pen and Sword titles please contact
Pen and Sword Books Limited
47 Church Street, Barnsley, South Yorkshire, S70 2AS, England
email: enquiries@pen-and-sword.co.uk
website: www.pen-and-sword.co.uk

CONTENTS

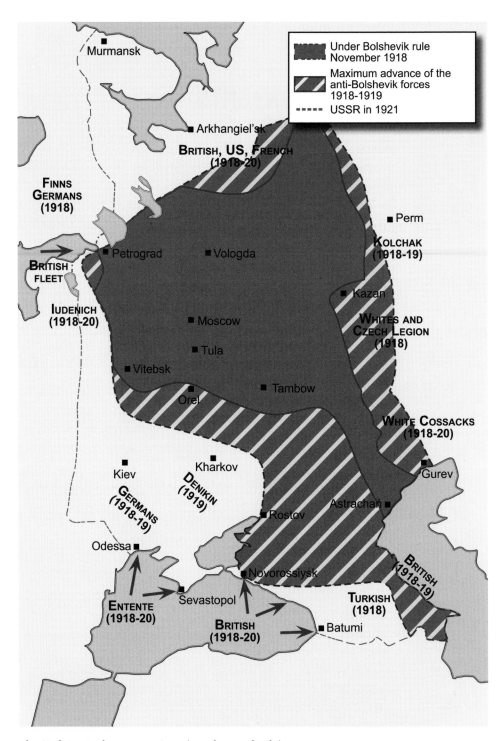

The Civil War in the West, 1918–21. (Map by Hoodinski)

TIMELINE

1917

26 February: Bakeries in Russia run out of bread leading to strikes. Petrograd becomes an armed camp with soldiers firing on the crowds but some soldiers start joining the demonstrations.

15 March: The Tsar orders the military to end the dispute but after many of the Russian military joined the striking civilians in Petrograd, Nicholas II is forced to abdicate. A provisional government is formed under Kerensky.

30 April: The Tsar and the Royal family is handed over to the Ural Soviet at Ekaterinburg.

7 November: Bolsheviks led by Lenin storm the Winter Palace in Petrograd.

1918

19 January: Bolshevik troops invade the Assembly, forcing out the Socialists and other political parties.

9 February: Russia and Germany sign the treaty of Brest-Litovsk ceding Russian territory to Germany in return for an end to the fighting, much to the anger of the Allies.

5 March: German forces enter Russia and the Russian capital is moved from Petrograd to Moscow.

26 March: Trotsky appointed War Commissioner as the Red Army is increased dramatically in size

10 April: The first major battle between the Red and White armies take place at Yekaterinodar. The commander of the White Army, General Lavr Kornilov, is killed and General Anton Ivanovich Denikin takes over command of the White forces.

4 July: The all-Russian Congress of Soviets meets and adopts a Soviet constitution.

16 July: Abdicated Tsar Nicholas and all the royal family are murdered at night. The Red Army is believed to be responsible.

30 August: Lenin is shot by Fanny Kaplan while delivering a speech to the Socialist Revolutionary Party. Lenin survives as reprisals against political opponents escalate.

5 September: The White army, aided by the Czechs, is defeated by the Reds at the battle of Kazan.

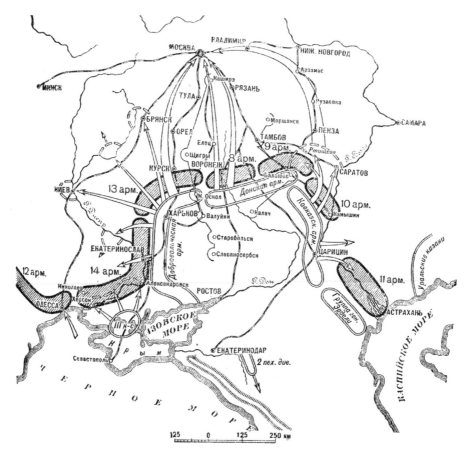

A 1934 map showing the dispositions of the Red and White armies during the latter's Moscow offensive in the summer of 1919. (A Egorov)

11 November: The First World War ends and the Germans leave Russia to be replaced by the Bolsheviks.

18 December: France sends troops to Odessa to aid the Whites in the civil war. Other Allied troops released from the war against Germany follow.

1919

19 March: U.S. officials meet with the Bolshevik leaders in Moscow.

9 April: The Red Army takes Odessa from Allied troops and the Whites.

13 October: After some success in Ukraine, the White army attempts to invade Petrograd but is unsuccessful.

1920

7 November: The battle of Perekop results in another Red victory, a significant point in the ending of the civil war.

INTRODUCTION

The Russian Revolution is often attributed to events concerning the First World War but the reasons date from much further in the past. The Russian Empire had its origins in the 18th century when it began to absorb neighbouring territories. It expanded as other empires around it declined such as the Swedish, Polish Lithuanian, the Persian and the Ottoman. It was eventually to become one of the largest empires ever to exist, stretching across three continents. The population varied enormously across the wide-ranging parts of the empire with a number of different ethnicities and religions all under control of the Tsar. It relied mainly on an agricultural economy which could often lead to periods of famine.

Although it was a major European power, the condition of its people was often poor in relation to their European neighbours. Slavery was legal in Russia well into the 19th century and people could be sold as servants or workers; even after a law was passed changing the status of slaves to serfs, it was still possible to sell landless serfs by advertising them as servants for hire. All this led to numerous revolts and assassination attempts during the 19th century. There was the ubiquitous secret police force that was used to combat this and countless people were executed or sent to Siberia.

Russian had become a major European power by the 19th century and played a large part in the defeat of Napoleon especially after he attempted to invade Russia in 1812 and was done in as much by the Russian winter as by the Russian army. But it was another war that made the need for reform in Russia so urgent. The Russian army in the Crimean War was sub-standard, seen by some as a reflection of the general population and the inability of the country to develop an industrial base.

The need for reform was understood by intellectual movements within the empire. Serfdom was eventually abolished in 1861 when the serfs became full citizens and were given the right to marry without consent and to own property. Landowners however lobbied relentlessly that freed serfs should not be allowed to own land: they needed cheap labour to work their estates.

By the time of the abolishment of serfdom however, many large estates were mortgaged to the state or to banks. Peasants could buy their land from the landowner with the government paying 75 percent of the price. They would still have obligations to the landowner and have to pay back the government. Although now supposedly free, peasants could not then leave their land to work in factories. They had to all intents and purposes become sharecroppers, still prisoners to the aristocracy. Another result

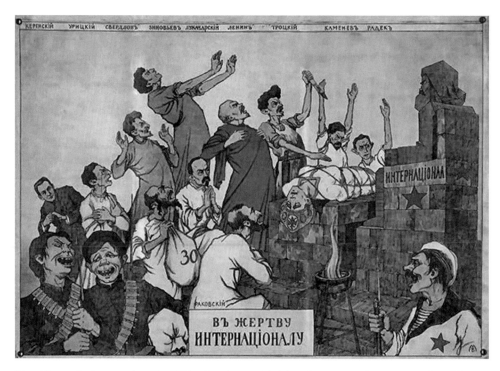

"Sacrifice to the International", a White Russian anti-Bolshevik propaganda poster produced during the Russian Civil War. In this image, a number of senior Bolsheviks—Uritzky, Sverdlov, Zinoviev, Lunacharsky, Lenin, Patrovsky, Trotsky, Kamenev and Radek—sacrifice an allegorical character representing Russia to a statue of Karl Marx. The figure of Alexander Kerensky can be seen behind these figures, looking on impotently. In the foreground are negative stereotypes of Red Army characters, a sailor, Jews, one of whom holds a bag of thirty pieces of silver, a reference to the Biblical figure of Judas Iscariot, and Asiatic soldiers with booty.

Red Guards warm themselves on the streets of Petrograd, November 1917. (Yakov Vladimirovich Steinberg/Adam Szelągowski)

Moscow street children
during the civil war.

of the reforms was to create local government of a fashion. This went some way to
weakening the idea of autocracy that had always been the form of government at
the core of the Empire. Local changes were not always what the Tsar had in mind
and there were often attempts to backtrack on the reforms that had previously been
promised. Despite the changes food production on the newly owned peasant farms
did not increase significantly and many did not have enough land to live off while
still having to work for the landowners. There were further cases of famine which
made the peasants believe that nothing had really changed for them. This led in many
cases to criticism of the new system and there were numerous cases of uprisings.

For those who did not work on the land conditions were just as bad. Hopes for
growth in industry since the reforms of the mid-nineteenth century faded. By 1917
there were still less than four million workers in Russia's factories and mines. The
difference between these workers and the peasants was that the urban workers were
concentrated in far larger groups and could thus present a greater threat to the ruling
class. Just as the peasants on the land were unhappy with their lot so were the factory and mine workers. They lived in terrible conditions and were forced to perform
monotonous tasks for very low wages.

Another difference between the peasants and urban workers was the opportunity
for education that was more accessible in the cities. Education meant that these workers became open to the new, subversive ideas of political reform. Factory workers
had a weapon that the peasants on the land did not have: the strike. The old way of
dealing with troublesome peasants still remained the favourite method of those in
control and their reaction to strikes and demonstrations was to send in the Cossacks
and the police.

A British airman trying out his Bristol fighter, Bakharitza, 6 September 1918. (US DoD via IWM)

One of the major turning points in the likelihood of revolution in Russia came during the Russo-Japanese war of 1904. The majority of the population had no idea what the war was about and the unexpected defeat led to problems at home and the near success of a revolution. It had become obvious that the Tsar's government was willing to use extreme violence against its own people.

The conflict between autocratic government and the people of Russia had then been a problem for many years before the First World War began. The revolution was a result of this but the war helped to create a situation where revolution became possible and more likely to succeed.

The revolution led not to a peaceful changeover of government but to decades of conflict and terrible suffering for the people of Russia. Millions died from starvation and violence as the revolution—instead of improving the life of the people—set them at each other's throats in a civil war that made the previous Tsarist violence seem benign.

There was a clear Allied view of the Russian Revolution published in *The Great War* magazine 27 April 1918: "The conflict between the extremists and the moderate revolutionary parties was energy that should have been exerted against the German invaders of Russia." According to the report the conflict had the character of a civil war that led to the breakup of the Russian Empire into a welter of semi-independent states.

1. BACKGROUND

Europe in the 18th century was to undergo a number of major upheavals that were to affect the lives of its entire people from the poorest to the richest and most powerful. One of the first major events was the French Revolution that erupted in 1789. Its effects were to resonate throughout Europe, and across the world, for decades to come. It resulted in a widespread continental and intercontinental war that involved almost all of Europe, and North America, and that was to last for almost thirty years, altering the balance of power, both domestically and internationally, forever.

The ruling classes of France were swept away and the fear of the same happening in the rest of Europe led to a series of alliances against Napoleon's France as royal families and ruling elites came together in a series of alliances and ententes to protect their positions. It was the unification of Europe that eventually put an end to Napoleon and reinstated the monarchy in France. However, the idea of revolution did not die with the return of French royalty, as witnessed by the continent-wide outbreak of uprisings in 1848.

Russia was one of Europe's major powers at this time. The Russian foreign minister, Rostopchin, is quoted: "Russia much by her position as to her inexhaustible resources is and must be the first power in the world." Europe was alarmed, fearing that Russia might engulf the whole of Europe, much as France had done under Napoleon. After all, was it not the Russian Bear that had brought the greatest military strategist since Alexander the Great to his knees?

Events in France, though a warning to Europe, did not actually set in motion a chain of events that were to affect the rest of the Continent. Western Europe, though writhing through the growing pains of the industrial revolution, was to take a very different path from that of Eastern Europe, and Russia. Britain led the way in development, with a swing from an agricultural economy to an industrialized power, with a corresponding leap in population growth and migration to the urban centres. The rest of Western Europe was not far behind with France, Belgium, Holland and Germany beginning to catch up as the century progressed. There were great changes in the way people worked and lived. Working hours no longer depended on daylight or the seasons. Factories had their own pattern of work and people had to be on time and stay at their work stations for as many hours as they were employed to work, often twelve or more hours a day, overseen by harsh foremen and their factory owners. However, the increase in population in the cities was not matched by development in housing and living conditions for most workers were dire, their being often worse off than they had been in the countryside. The main feature of the industrial

Nicholas II succeeded to the throne in 1894. He eventually replaced the Grand Duke Nicholas as commander of the forces in the First World War but was unable to lead them to victory.

revolution was technology: the use of iron and steel and new energy sources such as coal to power the steam engines that drove the new machines. This led to the factory system which increased the division of labour that could produce goods much faster and in greater numbers than the old system. The development of a large urban-based working class might have occurred in Western Europe but in the east in places such as Russia it didn't. Here economies were still agrarian with industrialization sluggish.

As well as a growth of the working class in the west, there was also an expanding middle class: these two classes had similar goals in attempting to reduce the autocratic control of the old aristocracy and ruling elites. The working class were becoming more politically aware with the ideas put forward by men such as Karl Marx. By 1848 Europe was once again inflamed with revolts breaking out in all the major continental cities. Thousands died and many were exiled but the Year of the Revolutions was to have a lasting effect.

Revolts against monarchies broke out in Sicily and spread to France, Germany and Italy. Serfdom was ended in both Austria and Hungary. The Hapsburg Empire, ruled from Vienna, was riven with attempts to gain autonomy by the subject races. The absolute monarchy in Denmark ended. In France the constitutional monarchy of Louis Phillipe came to an end. Although revolution in the German states was suppressed, it did have some effect in moving the country toward a unified Germany.

One of the Tsar's crack regiments. Unfortunately the Russian army did not perform well in the Crimean War, the Russo-Japanese War or the First World War.

Some countries were little affected by the revolutions such as Britain where there was a small-scale Chartist movement and some trouble in Ireland. In Belgium and the Netherlands there were peaceful reforms. Some countries were not affected at all: Spain, the Scandinavian countries and most importantly Russia.

The widespread unrest that had swept across Europe had seen many heads of states swept away and although Russia was barely affected, the warning signs were there for the Tsar to see but he refused to heed them, believing that his rule was based on the power given him by God: the Divine Right of Kings. It was a sign of how the Russian monarchy was to deal with a series of threats throughout the 19th century and into the next.

However, until his death in 1881, there had been some limited reforms under Alexander II including the setting up of two institutions that seemed totally out of place in Russia: the Zemstvos which administered schools, roads and public health in the countryside and the Dumas who did the same but in the cities. They were left in place by the tsars after Alexander but were under the control of autocratic bureaucrats; the people had little influence on what decisions were made by these bodies. There were even policies put in place toward the end of the 19th century that went some way toward reversing the earlier reforms and taking back some of the control that had been given at local district level.

The situation in Russia at the beginning of the 20th century was vastly different from much of the rest of Europe where there had been some movement toward empowering the masses. Tsar Nicholas II had more power than any other person in the world at that time, with over 130 million subjects under his control. He was blind to any other political system except his own feudal autocracy. The power of the Tsar was exercised through an enormous nepotistic bureaucracy of ministers and governors, many of whom were members of the Tsar's own family. The powers these men held were enforced by a plethora of police forces across the empire: political police, city police, rural, railway and factory police as well as the regular police force. The fact that so many police forces were seen to be needed would seem an obvious sign that there was a problem in the way the country was run.

Despite the ruthless control exercised by the Russian ruling class, there were many seen as likely to be the cause of trouble within the empire, mainly among the many groups of non-Russians that fell within the sphere of Tsarist rule such as in Finland, Poland and the Baltic States, perhaps understandable after the problems with non-Russians which had led to the assassination of Alexander II in 1881. Urban working classes were also seen as hotbeds of unrest.

Although Alexander II had been known as 'The Liberator' for his reforms, there was still widespread unrest because of his ruthless political policies. For example,

The Russian royal family and their bodyguard taken just before the revolution. The Tsar is in the centre with his son on his left.

in 1863, he brutally suppressed a rising in Poland when hundreds of Poles were executed and thousands sent to Siberia. At the same time martial law was declared in Lithuania which was to last forty years.

Despite his reforms Alexander was assassinated in 1881 when bombs were thrown at his carriage, an armoured carriage that had been a gift from the French. The first grenade did him little harm but as he got out of the carriage another exploded, critically injuring him. He did not die immediately but later that same day. His successor, Alexander III, immediately tried to clamp down on subversive elements with the introduction of further police force.

There was also another group within the empire that was problematic, the Jews, long seen as enemies of Christianity and the most likely to foment revolution. Propaganda propounded that Jews exploited the peasants, which was patently untrue but which suited the landed classes. The Jews of Russia consisted of around half the world's Jewish population and this despite years of persecution and regular pogroms. Most of them lived in Poland, inherited by Russia in 1795 when Poland was dismembered and shared out between Austria, Prussia and Russia,

Russia itself had a large Jewish population that went back centuries. They were restricted to living in certain areas and did not enjoy the rights of other citizens. In 1827, however, they were permitted to serve in the Russian army. This still did not stop the discriminatory treatment and in 1891, for example, the majority of Jews

The Grand Duke Michael whom the Tsar nominated as his successor but who refused the crown.

in Moscow were expelled from the city. Government policy toward the non-Russian and the Jewish populations within the empire was assimilation which in many cases promoted the actual anti-Russian feeling they were trying to remove. This in turn led to stricter measures being enforced which simply exacerbated the matter. The Pale of Settlement was a western region of the Russian Empire that existed from 1791 to 1917. This was where Jews were allowed to live. However, they were even excluded from some urban centres within the Pale. A few more affluent or educated Jews were allowed to live outside the Pale.

However, Russia's main problem at the time was its backwardness in terms of industrialization. More than a 100 million Russians relied on agriculture for their living. After the abolition of serfdom in 1861, much later than in the rest of Europe, peasants were afforded allotment land to farm: however, there was no land ownership by the peasants—and consequently no collateral for farming subsidies and loans—as the land was owned by the local 'commune', itself owned by the aristocracy or the government.

The farm allotments were not large enough to feed a family and the peasants had to supplement their income by working for landowners. There appeared no solution to the growing number of peasants without upsetting the existing social order which was strongly resisted by the landowning classes. Reforms were therefore ineffectual. The government did go some way in trying to improve the lot of those people working in industry although numbers were still minute when compared with those on the land— around three million at the turn of the 20th century. Reforms were paltry: restrictions were placed on the hours that children could work and fines that employers could set on their workers were reduced. Strikes became the only way that urban workers could fight back and were to become the main weapon of the masses against the government

Right: A cartoon showing Russian hypocrisy toward the Jews who were relentlessly persecuted but would be asked for loans.

Below: Russian soldiers showing their loyalty to the Tsar by kneeling in his presence. Despite the devotion of his men, he managed to eventually turn them against him.

2. EMBRYONIC YEARS

Revolts and uprisings in Russia were not confined to the 20th century: unrest had been ongoing for centuries. The 17th century boasted a period known as the Time of Troubles when a number of revolts took place. There was also a serious famine between 1601 and 1603 when up to a third of the population died. As with revolts famine was also a common occurrence, and often the trigger for rebellion.

The Time of Troubles occurred between the death of the last Russian Tsar of the Runk Dynasty, Feodor Ivanovich, in 1598 and the establishment of the Romanov Dynasty in 1613. As well as several uprisings the Polish-Muscovite War took place between 1605 and 1616 when a significant portion of Russia was occupied by the Polish-Lithuanian Commonwealth.

One of the more serious revolts of the Time of Troubles was the Bolotnikov Rebellion of 1606. Bolotnikov raised a small army consisting of escaped serfs, criminals and other unsavoury characters. Bolotnikov had a colourful background, once being a slave on a Turkish galley until freed by a passing German ship. He promised to eliminate the ruling classes of Russia and had some early success. There were a number of other small revolts going on at the same time in a similar fashion to what happened in the Russian civil war, only in 1606 the divergent groups united. The battle of Kromy in August 1606 saw the Russian army defeated. Bolotnikov's army then besieged Moscow but his allies began to melt away when the siege was lifted. After a final victory at Kaluga, he was captured at Tula in 1607 and executed. The Tsar had promised to pardon the rebels but once they surrendered he went back on his word and executed the lot.

The Bashkir Rebellion took place in 1662–64. The Bashkir tribes lived on the left bank of the Volga and rebelled after harsh treatment by Russian officials and the seizure of land by the Tsarist government. Led by some prominent lords, the Russian army struggled to put down the rebellion with concessions being made to resolve the issues. In 1681 jihad was declared by the Bashkir after it was rumoured that all non-Russian subjects were to be forced to become Christians. There were a number of similar revolts by Muslim tribes over the years, in Russia's ongoing programme of enforced assimilation.

Even the Russian military was not averse to voicing their anger at the Tsar. In 1825 the Russian army had pledged allegiance to the new Tsar Constantine. However, when Constantine renounced the right to succession, essentially removing himself as Tsar, Nicholas I was appointed Tsar instead. A number of army officers were

Apart from Russians, the Russian Empire contained a wide variety and diversity of ethnic groupings. Here are some Lazian militia, from the Black Sea area.

opposed to this and gathered in St Petersburg in December to protest. Around 3,000 men gathered in St Peter's square to protest against the new Tsar, faced off by 9,000 loyal troops. Shooting broke out before the Tsar sent Count Mikhail Miloradovich, a famous war hero, to address the rebels but he was shot dead. At the same time a force of rebel Grenadiers tried unsuccessfully to enter the Winter Palace. An attempted loyalist cavalry charge failed to disperse the rebels so artillery was brought forward that left many dead and subsequently ended the revolt that became known as the Decembrist Revolt. Some of those involved in the Decembrist Revolt became martyrs who inspired successive generations of dissidents. A number of them were members of secret revolutionary societies such as the Union of Salvation, the Union of Welfare, the Northern Society and the Southern Society.

The situation had not changed much by the beginning of the 20th century with the constant threat of revolt and revolution presiding over the country. By 1904 there had been a serious increase in opposition to the government, much of which was led by students as workers and peasants alike saw them as the best way to express their discontent.

The students themselves were often aided or directed by those who had fled the country after the unrest of the 1880s. The first Russian Marxist group—the Group for the Liberty of Labour—had been formed in Switzerland in 1883, In 1897 Lenin went into exile for three years for illegal worker activities. The number of opposition organizations was, however, enormous and could basically be divided into two

A St Petersburg street demonstration that was to become more and more common and that increasingly included disillusioned soldiers.

groupings: the revolutionary aimed at violent overthrow of the government and those hoping to gain liberty by peaceful means.

Lenin spent some time in London where he was able to read Karl Marx for the first time. There was a large Russian émigré contingent living in the east end of London, many of them members of the Anarchist Club in Jubilee Street in Stepney. Many of these were revolutionaries rather than anarchists and a large number of them were Jewish.

The most famous incident involving these anarchists was the Sidney Street battle in 1911 when a number of Latvian anarchists robbed a jewellers in Houndsditch and then fought a pitched battle with the police and the army from a house in Sidney Street which led to the use of artillery. There would seem to be little doubt that Lenin must have come into contact with some of these people during his time in London. A committed enemy of Bolshevism was present at the Sidney Street battle, Winston Churchill.

Another reason for the growth in opposition to the Tsar in the 20th twentieth century was the growth of literacy in the country. The number of literate peasants in Russia doubled between 1899 and 1914 although it was still only around 40 percent of the population. The French revolution and the British industrial revolution had occurred when the literacy levels were approaching 50 percent so perhaps this was a warning that the Russian government should have foreseen what was to come.

The reaction of the government to the opposition was mainly enacted through Vyacheslav von Plehve who had investigated the assassination of Alexander II and who had been made minister of the interior in 1902 after the assassination of his predecessor, Dmitry Sipyagin. Much of the information collected on the revolutionary movements in the country came from secret agents of the political police controlled by Plehve.

Previous revolutionary movements in Russia had faded without having had any lasting effect and the latest movements could have gone the same way without any serious results had it not been for one event, the 1904–05 war with Japan. The Tsar had expected an easy victory over the Asian race but as one defeat followed another, the morale of the people at home began to decline. With the Russian Pacific Fleet almost annihilated by the Japanese, there was little understanding among the population as to what the war was even about.

The country had only recently begun to recover from the economic depression of the turn of the century. Many industries struggled during the war and employment levels declined. The political awakening of the Russian people began to spread within the army. Despite the Tsar's poor treatment of his non-Russian subjects, many Poles were fighting in the Russian army along with large numbers of Jews which seemed to prove conclusively to the Tsar that they were patriotic to the Russian state despite their appalling treatment

Japanese troops stop for a lunch of rice and tea on their way to the front to fight the Russians, 1904.

What looked to be an easy war against the Japanese proved to be anything but. The Russians had the use of Port Arthur, leased from China, but needed another Pacific port to exert influence over Manchuria and Korea. The Japanese were worried about Russian expansionism in the region which they saw as a threat.

Japan offered to recognise Russian dominance in Manchuria in exchange for recognition of Korea being within the Japanese sphere of influence. Russia however wanted Korea north of the 39th parallel to be a neutral zone between Russia and Japan. Japan had already fought a war with China in 1894 to exert influence over Korea. In 1896 King Gojong of Korea fled to the Russian legation in Seoul because he believed that his life was in danger from Japanese agents which then led to growing Russian influence in Korea. Japan decided to go to war instead of carrying on with negotiations. Russia had pressured China into granting them the lease for Port Arthur. This was after it had previously forced Japan to relinquish the same right after Japan had defeated China in the war of 1894-95.

The Russians had a military entente with France at this time but the French said that it only applied to Europe so would not participate in any conflict with the Japanese. The Tsar also believed that Germany would support him. Meanwhile the British shared information with the Japanese and nearly got involved in the war when Russian ships attacked British fishing boats from Hull believing them to be enemy craft.

The Japanese made the first move and attacked Port Arthur in February 1904. The Russians had built fortifications above the harbour that the Japanese took using artillery in spite of enormous losses suffered by the Japanese troops. The Japanese then used artillery to destroy the Russian ships in the harbour that could do little to retaliate against the shore attack. The Russian ships were unable to leave the port because of a blockade by the Japanese navy.

The first land battle took place at the Yulu river in May and again the Russians were stunned by a defeat, despite large Japanese losses against strong Russian defences. The Russian army was soundly defeated again at the battle of Mukden in February 1905. The rest of the world was as shocked as the Russians at the defeat of a western power by an Asian country. It did not stop there as another Russian fleet was destroyed at the battle of Tsushima.

The Russians had expected to easily win the war and it was the first defeat of a European army by an Asian one in centuries. The Russians, like all Europeans, had

Russian troops mobilize during the war with the Japanese, 1904.

nothing but contempt for the Japanese but all Asians. The Russian troops treated the Chinese population very badly during the war, often killing and raping civilians, believing erroneously that because they were Asian they would support the Japanese. Quite naturally the Chinese became more inclined to support the less aggressive Japanese.

The handling of the war by the Tsar shows a complete lack of understanding of the situation, both abroad on the battlefield and domestically at home. There are suggestions that the Tsar instigated the war to promote Russian nationalism at home but the result was the exact opposite. There is also a view that he was trying to bully the Japanese as he did not think that they would go to war against a vastly superior nation with a better navy and army. It seems that his advisers held the same view; it is an example of how the Tsar continuously depended on men who were in the position they were due to their societal status rather than merit, something that came home to roost during the First World War.

It was evident that Russia was still capable of sending more troops to fight the Japanese, but there were serious problems with the economy and unrest among the

Japanese troops preparing to deploy to the front, 1904.

Vodka rations distributed to the sailors of the Imperial Russian Navy ship *Rossiya*, pre-First World War.

people at home. Even had Russia managed to win the war, it would have been irrelevant to the masses. The Tsar seemed to have continued the war as long as he did rather than admit to a humiliating defeat.

There seems little doubt that Nicholas held the Japanese in contempt no doubt because they were not European but it ultimately became evident that the Russians were unable to win the war and the Tsar's decision to sue for peace was influenced primarily because of domestic unrest and the surge in the subversive movement.

This did not prove as quite simple as he first thought. During a peaceful protest by workers in Petrograd the Tsar's forces acted in the only way they knew how and attacked the crowd of innocent protestors.

3. SUPPRESSION

In July 1904 Plehve was assassinated. The murder of government officials was not unusual at this time but the minister of the interior was a high-profile target. His death was celebrated by many because of his repressive policies. There had been attempts on his life before, one in 1903 and two in 1904, before the successful one when a bomb was thrown into his horse-drawn carriage.

Plehve had been a target for Jewish revolutionary groups. He had put forward a proposal to the Tsar about making a request to the Turks for permission for the Jews to colonize Palestine, an idea he believed Russian Jews would embrace because of the discriminatory practices in place against them. However, he had done nothing to supress a wave of anti-Jewish violence in 1903. Anti-Semitic pogroms had begun in earnest after Russia had acquired the territories of Eastern Europe and by the early 20th century had become routine. For example, after the 1905 October Manifesto, some 600 pogroms of varying size and intensity took place.

The Manifesto was the Tsar's unwilling reaction to the unrest. It was supposed to give the population the franchise to form an elected Duma that had to approve new laws. The Tsar had preferred to dispense with any form of government altogether

When the revolts of 1904 erupted protestors built barricades to block streets in Moscow.

Another Moscow street barricade.

and declare martial law to deal with the unrest but the Grand Duke Nicholas threatened to shoot himself if the Tsar did not sign the Manifesto.

Prior to this, by November 1904 a congress had been formed. There were calls for
freedom of the press and of speech, religious freedom and the right of association
and assembly. Today such rights are taken for granted but for the Russian populace
of the time they were unheard-of hopes.

The beginning of 1905 saw a dramatic increase in the pressure on the Tsar. There
had been a number of strikes with workers planning and a large march on the Winter
Place, to be led by a priest, Father Gapon. The aim of the assembly was for a more
democratic government. It was hardly the most radical request or a dangerous movement but the Tsar saw any criticism of his rule as just that.

Father Gapon was the son of a peasant but he had been educated in a theological
seminary. He later became a teacher at a children's orphanage and in 1902 a priest in
St Petersburg. He had much sympathy for the poor who worked long hours in terrible
conditions. However, there were rumours that Gapon liked gambling and drinking;
there were also claims that he had assaulted a twelve-year-old girl. These rumours
were probably circulated to discredit him but the people saw him as a saintly leader.
He had formed the Assembly of Russian Workers in 1903 which had 9,000 members
within a year including hundreds of women despite the assembly having no policies for women workers. Wages for workers were already low but in 1904 prices rose
so high that they became untenable. Four members of the Assembly were sacked at
Putilov Iron Works and Gapon called for industrial action which led to strikes by

The Winter Palace in St Petersburg that dominates Palace Square has been the scene of so many poignant moments in Russian history.

more than 100,000 workers. The Tsar reacted in his usual way by strengthening the garrisons with more troops.

Gapon decided to make a personal appeal to the Tsar asking for a reduction in working hours, an increase in wages and an improvement in working conditions. He also went much further than industrial requests in demanding an end to the war with Japan and universal suffrage. The petition was signed by more than 150,000 people.

Not all dissidents agreed with Gapon's approach. Those in the Bolshevik and Menshevik* parties thought that the march on the Winter Palace would be a step toward revolution, believing that the Russian people were not ready for this and tried to dissuade Gapon against it. Some believed him to be mad.

On January 8 workers began to march from various parts of the city to meet at the Winter Palace where Gapon would present the petition. The crowd also consisted of the workers' wives and children. The marchers found their way blocked by the police and the army. When the marchers failed to stop the soldiers opened fire into the crowd. Gapon himself described how the group he was leading was attacked by Cossacks slashing at the crowd with their swords.

Government attacks took place at a number of routes the marchers were taking. Many of the marchers were carrying images of the Tsar to prove their loyalty. Most did not want to topple the government or the royal family but simply wanted better living conditions. Some marchers did in fact reach the square at the Winter Palace but Palace troops then opened fire on them. The day became known as Bloody Sunday. There were ninety-six deaths and over 300 wounded. Another thirty-four died from their wounds.

---

* The non-Leninist wing of the Russian Social Democratic Workers' Party.

DISCOVER MORE ABOUT MILITARY HISTORY

Pen & Sword Books have over 4000 books currently available, our imprints include; Aviation, Naval, Military, Archaeology, Transport, Frontline, Seaforth and the Battleground series, and we cover all periods of history on land, sea and air.

Keep up to date with our new releases by completing and returning the form below (no stamp required if posting in the UK).

Alternatively, if you have access to the internet, please complete your details online via our website at **www.pen-and-sword.co.uk.**

All those subscribing to our mailing list via our website will receive a free e-book, *Mosquito Missions* by Martin W Bowman. Please enter code number ACC1 when subscribing to receive your free e-book.

Mr/Mrs/Ms ....

Address...

....

Postcode.................................... Email address...

Stay in touch: facebook.com/penandswordbooks or follow us on Twitter @penswordbooks

Website: www.pen-and-sword.co.uk Email: enquiries@pen-and-sword.co.uk
Telephone: 01226 734555   Fax: 01226 734438

Freepost Plus RTKE-RGRJ-KTTX
Pen & Sword Books Ltd
47 Church Street
BARNSLEY
S70 2AS

The march was not a revolutionary one or even a rebellious one. The majority of Russian workers retained traditional conservative values of orthodoxy, faith in the government and with an entire indifference to politics. They believed that the Tsar would help them if they made him aware of their situation. The events of Bloody Sunday led to the ultimate disillusionment of Father Gapon. He left Russia and went to live in Geneva as other political emigrés had. He became one of those operating outside the country for change within it. He met Lenin and Plekhanov but had joined the Socialist Revolutionary Party. When he later returned to Russia he was suspected as an informer and was later found hanged in a cottage outside St Petersburg.

Martial law was declared in St Petersburg following Bloody Sunday. Groups of people deemed too large were dispersed by the troops. However, outbreaks of violence and strikes in many other parts of the country transpired over the following days. There were many who hoped that the anger of the population over Bloody Sunday might have led to an outright uprising but most of those able to lead such a movement were still outside Russia. Lenin stayed where he was. Trotsky was one of the few who did return to Russia but to little effect. And there was still no unified movement against the government that would have any effect.

The reaction of the Tsar was to meet a group of loyal workers from St Petersburg, window dressing in other words. He told them that the revolting workers had been misled by evil men and that in using force, innocent people had died because of them. He told the workers that he would do everything possible to improve conditions better. There was talks of reform but no action ever took place.

The year of 1905 was to be one of continuous strikes and sporadic outbreaks of violence in various parts of the country. The events in St Petersburg had provoked the public and there was a series of strikes in industrial centres, especially strong in Poland where 400,000 workers withdrew their labour. There were also strikes in Finland and on the Baltic Coast. The government reacted with its normal strong-arm methods and more than a hundred workers died in Poland. There was widespread street fighting in Odessa in June when martial law was declared. The unrest led up to a general strike in October that began in Moscow and spread throughout the country. In some parts the military joined in on the side of the dissidents. There were mutinies in the navy and the battleship *Potemkin* was hijacked and surrendered to Romania in return for asylum for the crew.

Patriotic movements sprang up, instigated by government or local officials. In Odessa where there had been so much violence in June, a patriotic demonstration was attacked by revolutionaries, many of whom were Jews. This led to widespread anti-Jewish rioting which led to many deaths. There were many other anti-Semitic demonstrations in the country and loyalist-versus-revolutionary riots.

A military parade in Vladivostok during the First World War. There was a sense of optimism when the war began, the presence of Allied flags showing loyalty to the common cause.

Despite the widespread violence and strike movement there was still no organized revolutionary movement to attempt an overthrow of the government. It appeared that the revolutionaries were nervous of taking a step in that direction, not fully confident of their abilities. In November the Tsar then acted and set his army on the provinces where the peasants were revolting. Troublemakers were deported to Siberia.

There was a general strike in December and the troops sent to deal with the problems used artillery to break up demonstrations and to shell workers' districts. It was believed that thousands died during the troubles of 1905 and many more were imprisoned before the situation was brought under control by the end of the year.

The Tsar had also sent troops into Moscow on 15 December to deal with a strike. About a thousand civilians died before the strike ended on 19 December. Many more were sent to Siberia. Opposition continued in some areas but it was obvious that the end of the movement was near and that there would be no real change.

Despite the fact that the country was teetering on the brink of revolution, the Tsar remained oblivious. He was more interested in "the weather, who came to tea and how many birds he had shot". He seemed too reliant on advisers who blamed the problems on foreign agents. It was as though he was being shielded from the severity of the situation and the real reasons for the opposition to his rule.

By early 1906 many regions of the country had been returned to direct government control. There was a similar movement in the cities after the strike leaders had been arrested. Newspapers were closed and in St Petersburg the leaders of the Soviet were arrested. The rebels reacted by calling another general strike which seemed to be their only weapon.

It is easy to criticize the Tsar as being unable to see what was actually going on in Russia but perhaps this was not just a Russian problem but a failure of those in power everywhere to recognize the need to listen to the desires of the masses. On 31 January 1905 the American ambassador to Russia, Robert Sanderson McCormick, wrote to Secretary of State John Hay about the events of Bloody Sunday. He claimed that the working men had been worked on by a group of Socialists and that Father Gapon had been raised by them to the position of a demigod. He went on to claim that Gapon had violated a young girl of twelve. He also claimed that Gapon's plan had been to take the Tsar hostage. McCormick's view seemed to be based entirely on gossip.

An official proclamation on the order of the Tsar was published in *The Times* on 27 January 1905. It said that the agitation occurring in St Petersburg was being taken advantage of by those evil people who chose the workmen for their tools. Such evil-disposed men led the workmen astray with demands that had nothing in common with the people's needs. The proclamation went on to say that the Russian government had always shown itself careful of the people's needs.

To claim this in the face of the suffering evident in Russia at that time makes one wonder if those responsible for its publication had any idea what the conditions

Lenin spent much of his time abroad, studying the works of Marx and formulating his ideology of a post-Tsarist Russia.

of the population were like. The Tsar did, however, make some concessions after the problems of 1905. The military had remained loyal as was shown in their willingness to fire on workers. Had they not been then perhaps the concessions would have been greater. The Imperial Duma was created. This was a lower house of a parliament which was able to pass laws. However, there was an upper house, the State Council of Imperial Russia which was dominated by nobles. The Tsar also kept his autocratic position by having a veto on any laws passed. Thus the Duma was in effect almost powerless.

Until 1905 political parties were illegal. After the 1905 uprisings political parties were unbanned and a number popped up, not all of them anti-government. The Conservative Union of the Russian People was organized by state officials and the Church and was loyal to the Tsar. Opposition parties were numerous but not unified in their aims. Although the Tsar had allowed the foundation of the Duma, he believed that the reforms of 1905 had gone too far. The Duma went through the motion of passing laws, but essentially the Tsar ruled by decree. Election laws were also changed to influence the composition of membership of future Dumas after the first one was dissolved by force in 1907. This resulted in reducing the influence of the working classes and gave more power back to the nobility. It seems the Tsar had learned little from the events of 1905 and had no real intention of giving any power to the people. It was obvious to the population that the Tsar's so-called reforms meant little: the struggle continued through strikes which were illegal but still happened, demonstrations and even troops refusing to obey orders and open fire on crowds. The more militant political groups took sterner action and the number of political assassinations occurring in Russia increased dramatically.

Despite the problems at home, Russia was also facing international difficulties. After the war with Japan, Russia had surrendered Port Arthur and relations with Britain improved because of this. In 1907 Russia and Britain agreed on Afghanistan becoming a buffer state between their empires, thus ending many years of suspicion between the two powers. It was an agreement which was to be forgotten after the revolution. However political problems in the Balkans in 1908 and the following Balkan Wars raised tensions between Russia and Austria. It was this that eventually played such definitive role in the outbreak of the First World War.

The relationship between Russia and Britain at the outbreak of the war was explained by Sir George Buchanan in his memoirs. He described them as being friends but not allies. As the certainty of war became evident in Russia there were continual requests on the British ambassador to state whether Britain would enter the war to support Russia against Germany, something that was not to be rushed by the British. There seemed some level of belief by the Tsar that if Britain pledged her support for Russia then there would be no war as Germany would back down.

A group of Russian soldiers with interesting variations in their uniforms. Some appear to be officers. It is unclear what the '39' flag represents.

Buchanan was still hoping that Britain could broker an agreement that would result in peace. He was hoping that if Russia did go to war then it could be seen that it was Germany and Austria who were the aggressors which might sway sway public opinion in Britain to support Russia. The Tsar did at one point, toward the end of July 1914, try to stop Russian mobilization to appear as a non-aggressor.

According to Buchanan there was also a belief in Germany that if there was a war that there would be a revolution in Russia which could then mean that Germany would not have to fight the Russians. The result was to be the opposite. When the Tsar appeared on the balcony of the Winter Palace on the day after Germany declared war against him the huge crowds waiting to see him fell to their knees singing the national anthem. The only violence to take place was an attack on the Germany embassy. Perhaps it was such events that reassured the Tsar that he was safe in the support of his people. There is no doubt that much of the population were devoted to the Tsar despite their appalling conditions. So much so that stamps issued with images of the royal family were withdrawn after post office staff refused to 'deface' with postmarks the faces of the royals.

Russian infantry in the First World War, all with their own rifles which was often not the case.

Tsarina Alexandra Feodorovna (Alice of Hesse-Darmstadt) with her sister Grand Duchess Elizaveta Fedorovna (Elisabeth of Hesse-Darmstadt).

4. WAR

The role of Russia in the First World War has often been ignored in favour of the events on the more newsworthy Western Front and the role of Britain, France and the Americans (when they arrived). The Russian Imperial army has long been considered inadequate to wage an industrialized war, despite its vast amounts of troops: the Russian army numbered more than six million men.

The Russians had already been aided by the Allies before the war, particularly the French and although this had significantly improved the railway system, the army still did not have a transport system that could supply such a large number of men, let alone mass-mobilize them to the fronts. Despite having millions of men under arms, the total number of motor vehicles in the army numbered only in the hundreds: the army was still mainly reliant on horse power.

There was, however, a feeling of optimism in Russia at the outbreak of war. They had increased military spending since the war with Japan and by 1914 were spending more than Germany on their armed forces. The Germans had been hoping, in vain, that it would take the Russians so long to mobilize that they could defeat France before turning to deal with the Russians.

Senior Russian officers posing outside their train on the South-Western Front.

The problem Russia faced was that it was only prepared for a short war, with no contingency plans for an extended conflict. The same could be said of their allies but France and Britain were more able to adapt; Russia was too inflexible and inefficient to do so. The War Department could not even provide the troops with boots after the first few months of the war as no one in the Commissariat had realized that they could not produce enough of them. And despite having the largest army in the world, more than six million, Russia's poor roads and rail networks made it problematic to mobilise them. The army only had just over four million rifles but the Tsar boasted the largest air force in the world with 360 aircraft and sixteen airships. The navy had four battleships, ten cruisers, twenty-one destroyers, eleven submarines and fifty torpedo boats.

When the Tsar visited the front one company he reviewed were kitted out with the best uniforms and weapons while those in the trenches—which he didn't see—were left with hardly any equipment at all. This seems to be another example of the Tsar not seeing what the real situation was and being given a very false picture of the capability of his army. The army was also seriously short of medical supplies and the levels of disease among the troops must have matched those of the Crimean or Napoleonic wars. There came a point during the war where the transport system, which, as mentioned, was mainly reliant on horse-drawn transport, broke down so irretrievably that the men at the front had no boots or winter clothing.

The Russian ship *Evstaffy* displays some serious gunfire damage. The Russian navy mainly played a defensive role during the war.

This First World War Russian poster boasts a large, well-equipped convoy of ambulances. In reality the Russian army had very few motor vehicles and army medical services were negligible.

When the war began the Russians found themselves fighting on two fronts, one against the Germans in East Prussia and the other against the Austro-Hungarians in Galicia, and despite some very early success in East Prussia, the Russians were subsequently badly mauled by the Germans which set them back for the duration.

The Russian Second Army attacked East Prussia in the southwest in August 1914 under the command of General Samsonov while the First Army under General Rennenkampf moved into the northeast. The plan was for the two armies to combine and attack the German Eighth Army under General Prittwitz. After some early Russian success, the German commander was replaced by Hindenburg and Ludendorff. Rennenkampf and Samsonov were not on the best of terms and were unaware of what each other was doing, a common problem in the Tsar's army where commanders were used to having their own way. On 28 August Samsonov's force was routed at Tannenberg with 30,000 killed and 95,000 taken prisoner. As a result Samsonov shot himself. The Russian First Army had failed to come to his support which was part of the reason for his defeat. The Allies believed that this could have resulted in the complete collapse of the Russian army but it was sheer numbers that kept Russia in the war at this point.

In September General Joffre asked the Russians if they had enough ammunition to meet the high rate of consumption and was told that they had. Then, in December,

Russian troops pose with Turkish colours captured at Erzurum in 1916. The Russian success led to the discovery of the Armenian genocide undertaken by the Turks.

the chief of staff at the ministry for war said that although Russia had enough men to cover their losses, they did not have enough rifles to arm them or enough shells for the artillery. They were trying to buy munitions from abroad and at the same time increase production at home. In some cases men had to wait unarmed until they could take the rifles from their fallen comrades.

The Russians had more success against the Austro-Hungarians except when they were supported by the German army. By early 1915 however, things had improved and there was a chance of the Russians breaking through into Hungary. To combat this the German Eleventh Army was secretly moved from the Western Front to prop up the Austro-Hungarians. In early May the Germans attacked at Gorlice and Tarnow and in pushing the Russians back they took 140,000 prisoners and captured more than a hundred guns which the Russian badly needed. The Russian Third Army was almost annihilated. Within months the whole of Russian Poland had been taken by the Germans. The Russians were again seen to have failed but while they were still fighting, they were keeping the enemy forces fixed, preventing them being moved to the Western Front and putting pressure on the Allies.

Once again though, what looked like a serious defeat was avoided and during the winter of 1915/16 Russian industry was stepped up to provide more resources for the army. According to Buchanan, "1916 saw a distinct improvement in the delivery of war material from abroad as well as from the factories at home". Russia's former enemy Japan was one of the countries supplying weapons to the Russians and there was even suggestion that Japanese troops might be sent to the front to aid the Russians.

There was also a move to get rid of some of the incompetent Tsarist officers who were in position due to their birth rather than their military prowess. The quality of those in positions of power had always been a problem where nobility superseded ability. On the southwest front Nikolai Ivanov was replaced by Alexei Brusilov. Brusilov had realized as early as 1914 that cavalry was obsolete in the era of the machine gun. This was despite being a cavalry officer himself and shows his understanding of modern warfare, not something that was understood by many senior officers of all sides. Historians portray him as the only Russian officer of the war who was capable of winning a battle. His innovative and relatively successful tactics were later copied by the Germans which must be seen as a compliment to him.

Brusilov was the son of a Russian general, of noble birth and had attended a military training school only open to the aristocracy. He had also visited other European military academies and had some understanding of western military tactics. He had been involved in the early Russian success in Galicia but was also present at the

Russian troops in a trench waiting for a German attack.

Tannenberg disaster. However, he had conducted an orderly retreat that saved much of the army. His ideas were frowned upon by most of the Russian general staff. His plan was for the Russians to attack on three fronts in June 1916, to coincide with the large offensives taking place on the Western Front. He decided to attack with all his armies on a wide front with no prolonged artillery barrage beforehand that would warn the enemy of the forthcoming offensive, something that also helped preserve the limited stocks of artillery shells.

In early June Brusilov's armies broke through the Austro-Hungarian lines on a wide front while two other attacks on narrow fronts were stopped. Although the enemy had a strong front, there was little in the way of reserves and the Russians were able to advance five miles on a twenty-mile front and took over 200,000 prisoners.

A Russian soldier with his wife. It is not clear if he is on leave or this was taken before he was mobilized. He does seem to possess a decent pair of boots.

The failure of the other Russian attacks and the inability to supply the advance with matériel and fresh troops led to the eventual failure of the offensive. While Brusilov's armies paused, German troops were moved into the area to bolster the Austro-Hungarians and the Russian attacks faltered. It was to be the last Russian success of the war. Despite some improvement in the level of Russian industry, there were never enough supplies for the army. Lack of decent transport meant that not only could the army not be resupplied but that the wounded could not be evacuated. The original commissariat problems were worse than ever: many troops still had no boots; supply had improved but quality was poor and the boots quickly fell apart. Some troops still did not have rifles.

The problems at the front led to severe criticism at home. There were patriotic organizations that did their best to help pack and send supplies to the front. Young women volunteered to work as nurses but it was obvious to the population that the problems ran deep and that the government could not cope with the war. There were even rumours of treason and that some prominent figures were in favour of Germany winning the war, including the Tsarina: a reason was the influence that Rasputin had over her, with many suspecting him of being pro-German.

According to Buchanan, after the 1905 uprisings following the Japanese war, the Tsar and Tsarina had lived in comparative retirement at Tsarkoe Selo and only came to St Petersburg for state or religious ceremonies. There were no more grand balls and the court no longer played a major role in the social life of the capital.

Prompted by the Tsarina, the Tsar eventually decided to take command of the army himself which, according to Buchanan, was because the Grand Duke's popularity was eclipsing that of the Tsar. This was along with attempts by Rasputin and others to discredit the Grand Duke by blaming him for the failures of the Russian army. It seemed that despite the direst problems at home and at the front, petty jealousies and bickering at the highest levels were undiminished.

There was an interesting comment on Rasputin in the memoirs of Sir George Buchanan. He refuted the rumour that Rasputin was in the pay of the Germans. He admitted, however, that Rasputin was financed by Jewish bankers and these bankers were German agents. He claimed that Rasputin did pass them classified information that he'd heard at court which no doubt was relayed back to the Germans. Whatever the truth of Rasputin's allegiances, the people believed that there were German sympathizers at the highest level of Russian society and anti-German feeling led to attacks on anyone who looked German, including anyone well dressed as most Russians could not afford decent clothes.

Although ostensibly Russia's ally during the First World War, this did not stop Britain from operating a ring of intelligence officers in the Russian capital of Petrograd: the name had been changed from St Petersburg, at the outbreak of war, as Petrograd sounded less German.

A British officer assisted by Russian soldiers gives a Russian deserter a chance to return to the front and save his honour ... and his neck.

This network had been in operation as early as 1916 and the reports the British received showed that the war was not going well for the Russians on the Eastern Front. Gathering information may not have been the only objective of the British intelligence officers working in Russia: it was rumoured that one of these, Oswald Rayner, had been present at Rasputin's murder. Those working for the British government before and during the revolution in Russia were to be the original members of the organization that was to become MI6. One such was Somerset Maugham. In 1928 he published a book called *Ashenden: Or the British Agent* based on his experiences as an agent. In it he writes on taking the job and was told, "If you do well you will get no thanks and if you get into trouble you'll get no help."

Grigory Rasputin, with the clear hint of lunacy about him. (Karl Bulla)

There is no doubt that the unpopularity of the Tsar among some elements of the population was further exacerbated by Rasputin's influence over the royal family. According to Buchanan who had personal dealings with the royal family, "the Empress was throughout inspired by the best of motives, the love of her husband and of her adopted country." He went on to say however that the same could not be said of those surrounding her who influenced her with suggestions that furthered their own ends. Although this may have included Rasputin, it was not exclusively aimed at him.

Rasputin was originally brought into the royal family's lives in 1908 to help the Prince Aleksei Nokolayevich, the royal couple's only son, who was a haemophiliac. He did help the boy but how he did this is conjecture. He was supposed to have some kind of power. He then became an adviser to the Tsarina. Having a peasant in such a high position was unacceptable to those surrounding the royal family, many of whom were family members, and there was widespread jealousy of Rasputin at all levels of society. Buchanan did however go on to say that the Tsarina was "a reactionary who wished to hand down the autocracy intact to her son".

Rasputin holding a séance for upper-class Russians. It was unclear what sort of power Rasputin possessed but it was thought to be some kind of mysticism.

With this in mind, she prompted the Tsar to appoint ministers sympathetic to this policy, regardless of their abilities.

Rasputin was murdered in late December 1917 and the uncertainty about his murder is similar to the uncertainty about his life. A number of Russian nobles were supposedly involved but their statements contradicted each other. It has been suggested that it was not only Russians who were responsible: a number of British agents in Russia at the time have been mentioned as not only being present at his death but playing a major part in it. According to Richard Cullen, these were Samuel John Gurney Hoare; Viscount Templewood—later an MP in the 1920s—who at the time of Rasputin's death was a high-ranking agent in Petrograd; Oswald Rayner, an army officer stationed in Petrograd; John Scale, a captain in the Royal Warwickshire Regiment, was also in Petrograd at the time; and lastly Stephen Alley, an engineer working in Petrograd and who had been recruited by military intelligence. The Tsar supposedly told George Buchanan that a young Englishman was involved in Rasputin's death, a fact that Buchanan strongly denied.

Rasputin had achieved worldwide notoriety. He was described as the "peasant's fakir" and "a sinister influence in Russia" in *The Times* in early January 1917. The report even went on to say how his death had been reported on more than one occasion but this time his body had been found on the banks of the Neva. He was also described as a favourite at court and of enjoying the patronage of the empress.

Despite the Tsar now being in command of the army, at the front things were not looking any better. As well as shortages at the front there were also shortages in Petrograd—especially bread—as the transport system was on the verge of total collapse. Trouble broke out in Petrograd, reported by a British correspondent, Arthur Ransome. Another British reporter working for *The Times* witnessed riots on the streets of Moscow where shots were fired. The distinction between reporter and intelligence officer was now blurred, effectively being one and the same.

In early 1917 Lenin returned to Russia. Waiting at the station in Petrograd along with his supporters was a group of Englishmen. Among these was a man who was to find fame in other areas but at this time was a reporter for the *Daily News*. Arthur Ransome might have later become better known as a writer but in the years following Lenin's arrival he was involved in espionage against the Russian revolutionaries while working for the British government. There were even rumours in the west that the leader of the extremists, Lenin, was not really Lenin at all, that he was a double who had taken Lenin's identity after Lenin had died in exile. The person's real name was given as Cederblum or Zederbaum who was said to be German. When this was discredited there were claims that Lenin was in the pay of the Germans, a claim that Kerensky was later quick to repeat.

The British were already taking a hand in trying to stop the trouble that they knew was heading for Russia. British agents in the U.S. had been keeping an eye out for Indian and Irish troublemakers but also Trotsky who was living in New York. When Trotsky's ship stopped in Halifax, Nova Scotia, on his way back to Russia he was arrested but with threats against British subjects living in Russia, he was soon released.

February 1917 was to see further violence in Russia. Bakeries in Petrograd were running out of bread despite there being plenty of flour in the countryside. The severe weather had disrupted the transport system so supplies were not getting through. People queued all night for a loaf of bread. The crisis was blamed mainly on the Germans and the Jews, the usual scapegoats, and of course the government.

There were strikes in Petrograd in late February when workers marched through the city until they clashed with the police. Cossacks were sent against the crowds but had little effect as they were now unwilling to use force against the people. It seems that the army was now less inclined to use force as they were themselves were equally as angry—and as hungry—at the situation. The lack of suppression led to greater crowds of workers taking to the streets in the days that followed.

A detail of Russian soldiers bar the way of would-be deserters. The man striding toward them is a British officer.

The army itself was ripe for revolution and when the workers took to the streets again in Petrograd the Tsarist state teetered as thousands of soldiers and sailors joined the workers. In one case Cossacks turned on the police: instead of attacking the demonstrators as they had been ordered, many of the troopers then joined them. Despite what was happening, those in command had no idea how serious the situation really was or chose to ignore it, much as they had done often in the past. When the Tsar was informed of the troubles in the capital he told General Khabalov, chief of the Petrograd military district, to use military force to put down the dissent by the next day.

In fact, while the trouble was going on, a reception for Allied delegates, described as "brilliant", was held by the Petrograd mayor and city council at the town hall. The principal members of the French, British and Italian delegations were presented with gold and silver bowls as souvenirs of their visit. Lord Milner said of the reception that their stay had been prolonged, not through differences of opinion, but because of the enormity of the task they faced: Great Britain and Russia getting to know one and other more intimately. The problems evident in the city were not mentioned.

By Sunday 26 February Petrograd had become a military camp. Clashes continued between workers and sympathetic soldiers and soldiers and police still loyal to the Tsar. There were several deaths, including soldiers who had switched sides. The following day it appeared that even loyalist troops were now refusing to fire on the crowds. The rioters then captured the city arsenal and armed themselves, by which time it was only the police who were still firing on the demonstrators, with almost all the army having declared for the people or having claimed neutrality.

The Tsar was informed and tried to get back to Petrograd which was impossible as the transport system had broken down completely. It seemed that only now did the Tsar realize how serious the situation was.

It also seemed that the rest of the world did not quite realize how bad things were. It was thought that the war had increased national growth in Russia and that there had been remarkable development in the years following the war with Japan. Along with the growth there had, it was believed, been constitutional reforms and *The Times* described the progress made in moral and national welfare to border on the miraculous. The view was that there was no reason to expect that there would be any decline in this maturing process. The optimistic tone of *The Times* then changed to explain that "rapid growth is a painful process so there should not be any astonishment at the present crisis". In fact there was very little real understanding of what was going on in Russia among the outside world. Reports in the British press were often wildly contradictory; despite the earlier claims of positive change, a few weeks later headlines were claiming that there were repressive measures being taken in the country.

Officers of the British Armoured Car Section hold up deserters on the Russian front. The transport is all horse-drawn.

In fact a report of the arrest of fifteen workmen including eleven members of the Central Industrial Munitions Committee of Petrograd on a charge of revolutionary conspiracy was said to have caused no surprise.

By the end of February, despite the visit of the Allied delegates a few weeks previously, it was still not fully evident to the world just how critical the situation in Russia was. *The Times* on 28 February reported on rumours of trouble in connection with the opening of the Duma but then went on to say that these were false: it wasn't only the Tsar who was blind to the evidence. The report went on to say that the most unpopular ministers refrained from appearing but an address to the army and navy attempted to assuage the military that their sufferings and exploits were appreciated and that all efforts were being made by the nation to help the armed forces to victory. The speeches went on, blaming previous ministers for the problems facing the country, and promises were made to improve the situation.

Despite the overwhelming evidence facing him, the Tsar still believed that the royal family could survive at the head of the Empire. He abdicated on his own behalf and that of his son in March, suggesting that he be succeeded by Grand Duke Michael Alexandrovich, his brother. The Duke seemed to have a better grasp of the situation facing the country than the Tsar and declined the crown.

A provisional government was formed which, surprisingly, was to be run by a liberal aristocrat, Prince Georgy Yevgenyevich Lvov, at the head of the Duma. The new government had a rival in the Petrograd Soviet that enjoyed the support of the people. Lvov's government tried to get the Soviet to form a coalition but ended up with a dual ruling system in which the Soviet held the real power. The man who was to play a huge part in the new government was a Duma member, Alexander Kerensky. He was a lawyer and a moderate Socialist, popular with the working class despite the fact that he came from a middle-class background. He was elected as vice-chairman of the Petrograd Soviet in March and later became a member of the provisional government. He then became minister of justice. When Lenin returned to Russia Kerensky tried to arrange a meeting with him to find out what he intended to do but Lenin refused to meet him. It was as minister of war that Kerensky ordered the disastrous attack on the Austrians and Germans in Galicia in June 1917. It ended as had other large attacks—in disaster—due to a lack of supplies, poor leadership and an army that no longer had a taste for war. This was difficult for Kerensky as he strongly believed that Russia should carry on fighting, a fact that led to Allied support.

Attempts to keep Russia in the war were becoming more difficult by the day. British troops in Galicia were assisting Russian counterparts in stopping desertions and forcing the would-be Russian deserters to return to the front. But it was hopeless. According to Buchanan, Russian soldiers toward the end of the war did

Captain Gerard (at right on the tracks with a cane), a Russian interpreter for the British, helping prevent Russian soldiers from deserting

A Russian orders group at the front, prior to an attack, May 1917. (Yakov Vladimirovich Steinberg via russianphoto.ru)

not understand what they were fighting for (similar to the situation in the Russo-Japanese War). The Russian soldier had been ready to lay down his life for the Tsar but once the Tsar had gone the country meant nothing to him. He had no loyal feelings beyond those to his own village. In May and June the Russian army was in a state of limbo, hopelessly unable of undertaking any serious military operations. There was little discipline as disloyal elements began to take control. Most troops were poorly educated and were taken in by German propaganda; fraternization with the enemy was encouraged by the dissidents and fighting the Germans no longer seemed so important.

5. REVOLUTION AND CIVIL WAR

It wasn't only men involved in the uprising: in late February thousands of female textile workers demonstrated in Petrograd, protesting against the price of bread, unaffordable even when it was available. More than 200,000 workers were on strike. Unlike other occasions when only the working class was involved, over the next few days the strikers were joined by the middle classes and students calling for an end to the war and for an end to the Tsarist government. On February 26 the army opened fire on protestors and the following day troops mutinied

By the beginning of March the number of soldiers who had joined the demonstrators had risen to 200,000. Crowds were by this time attacking police stations, destroying Tsarist vestments and even arresting officials. Despite this the government continued to try and enforce its will using force. There were attempts to keep

Troops assembling at the Winter Palace in the early days of the revolution, 1917.

the strikers away from the centre of Petrograd. Trams were stopped and soldiers were placed at crossings on the Neva. Workers from the mills and munition works however often managed to bypass the barriers. Members of the Duma had persuaded army commanders that only the abdication of the Tsar could result in the continuation of the war. They formed a government and Nicholas abdicated. The revolution had different meanings for different groups. The people saw the abdication as a sign of freedom, that they were now citizens. Many wanted the war to end. The new government however saw it as a way of achieving victory. The army saw it as a way of getting rid of unpopular officers often by lynching. The army did however have a new *raison d'être*: they were protecting the revolution. Factory workers reacted in a similar way to the soldiers and sailors: they returned to work and got rid of unpopular foremen and administrators. Factory rules were abandoned and committees were formed to represent workers' interests—eight-hour working days and higher wages—and run the factories.

It was through the Soviets that the people gave expression to what they saw as the revolution. And there were more than a 1,000 Soviets by October. It was these Soviets that tried to keep an eye on Lvov's government; Lvov himself was a landowner with a long history of service to the Zemstvos but these local government organizations were later shut down and taken over by the Soviets. There were some Bolsheviks who wanted the Petrograd Soviet to take over the government. The Soviet already controlled the army and transport infrastructure. At this time however the revolution

Revolutionaries and students attacking Tsarist police in Petrograd, March 1917. (*Illustrated London News/ Sketch*)

Students' militia arrest an under-
cover policeman, March 1917.
(Yakov Vladimirovich Steinberg)

The Red Army parades
through Moscow, 25 May 1918.
(Grigori Petrowitsch Goldstein)

Red Army troops, 1917.
(Albert Rhys Williams)

May Day demonstration in Minsk, 1917. (Eugeniusz Mironowicz/ Najnouszaja historyja Biełarusi)

Revolutionaries attacking Tsarist police, March 1917. (Edward Alsworth Ross)

was still seen by many as a tool destined to bring about democracy and the development of capitalism in Russia, not socialism.

There was still a belief amongst the Allies that Russia was becoming more stable and would continue taking their part in the war. The new government was seen to have the support of the army under Grand Duke Nicholas and General Alexeieff, the Chief of Staff. Order in Petrograd was believed to be mainly restored.

Outside Petrograd control was undertaken out by committees of public organizations who used their power to get rid of Tsarist officials and the police. They then took over the responsibility of maintaining order and organizing the food supply. This normally led to the Zemstvos becoming more democratic; however, this often meant that there were two sources of power in a town. It also meant that the national government had little control outside Petrograd and Moscow. There was also another problem in that the government wanted to continue the prosecution of the war while most of the population was demanding an early peace settlement. Kerensky was one of the main supporters of the war, determined to fulfil Russia's obligations to the Allies. Many of the rank and file did not agree with him and there were widespread desertions along with large numbers of troops who simply refused to fight. This was perhaps one of the reasons why the government could not last.

The Provisional Government with Prime Minister Prince Lvov fourth from the right in the front row.

Members of the British Armoured Car Section giving machine-gun instruction to Cossacks in an attempt to stop the Russian retreat.

In April Lenin returned to Russia. Until then the Bolsheviks were no more than a small group on the periphery of power. Lenin was convinced that the war would result in the end of capitalism in Europe. The Bolsheviks were seen by many as the party of the people even if many had little idea of what Marxism really was. Numbers swelled.

There was a widespread belief in the West that Jews were the main instigators of the Russian Revolution. It was believed that they were the true power-brokers within the Bolsheviks. This became a feature of the propaganda spread by the anti-communist White forces during the civil war.

Allied confidence in the continuing support of the Russians was soon seen to be based on shaky ground. In July members of the First Machine Gun Regiment, angry at continued failure in the war and not wanting to be part of it any longer, took to the streets and demanded that the Soviets take control of the government. There were still some regiments loyal to the government however—keeping the government in power—but the government's grip on the country was precarious. Kerensky accused the Bolsheviks of being German agents and ordered the arrest of many of them including Trotsky and Lenin. Lenin fled to Finland while others were jailed. The government's success was however short-lived: the economy began to decline as production fell and thousands of workers were laid off. Food was scarce and prices soared.

There was also trouble in the countryside. The government tried to buy grain from the peasants to feed the workers and the army but the peasants preferred to keep it. The peasants then began to seize land to graze their cattle and stole wood from landowners' forests. There was little the government could do about it as they had problems enough simply controlling the towns.

By this time Kerensky had become prime minister but there were many who felt that the only way to save Russia was a military dictatorship. Kerensky's knew there was a need for firm government. General Kornilov had been made supreme commander of the army: a clash between the general and Kerensky was inevitable when Kornilov demanded that military and civil authority be placed in his hands. Kerensky then tried to remove the general from his command but his troops had begun moving on Petrograd. When Kerensky called on the Soviets for help it opened the door for the Bolsheviks to make a comeback. Their slogan "All power to the Soviets" became a popular theme for the masses. Lenin returned in October. Despite this Kerensky clung to power and stayed on as prime minister but it was to be his insistence of keeping Russia in the war that was to lead to the eventual downfall of

The Women's Battalion of Death on parade at the Winter Palace, ready to defend the Provisional Government.

the government and to the eventual takeover by the Bolsheviks—who wanted no further part in the war—in October.

In early October the government had announced that half the garrison in Petrograd was to be moved out of the city to oppose the German advance. It was seen as an attempt to get rid of the revolutionary elements in the army. A Military Revolutionary Committee was formed to oppose the movement. When ordered to deploy the committee ordered the troops to stay put. Kerensky then ordered Bolshevik printing presses to be closed down before attempting to move against the Military Revolutionary Committee. Soldiers backed by armed workers took control of bridges, railway stations and other points. Lenin reappeared in public on 25 October 25. Only the Winter Palace remained in the hands of the government by this time.

The takeover of the government by the Bolsheviks was seen as a coup, the difference being that normally a coup is the takeover of a functioning state. Russia was not a functioning state and had not had one since February. The idea of democracy in Russia had proved unviable and short-lived.

The Great War magazine described Lenin as

Three members of the Women's Battalion of Death.

a revolutionary by profession, a man of unbalanced ideas, a fanatic of the narrowest type, who would turn the whole world upside down to realize his delusions. An exact parallel to him is to be found in the French Revolution in the anarchist Cloots who was equally destitute of humour and likewise held that nations are evil but the human race is good.

According to the writer Sergei Golitsyn, in the winter of 1917 many of the former privileged classes fled south and east from St Petersburg and Moscow, not out of fear of the revolution but from hunger. Those with country estates stayed on them, avoiding their houses in the cities. Many others managed to escape the country altogether, particularly to France.

The war and the revolution had led to widespread hunger and lack of fuel. The Bolsheviks were to proclaim that there would be equal distribution of goods and nationalization of industries but in practice this meant little. The new government had as little power in the countryside as had the last one and it was the peasants

Distribution of the *Izvestia* newspaper to military representatives at the Tauride Palace, March 1917. (Yakov Vladimirovich Steinberg)

Khralamov, a commissar of the Provisional Government, addresses the junkers in front of Alexander Nevsky Cathedral, Tiflis, Georgia, 19 May 1917 (National Archives of Georgia)

One of the earliest Red Guard regiments in Petrograd, autumn 1917. Most still wear civilian clothes.

The Winter Palace after the seizure by squads of the Soviet Military Revolutionary Committee, 8 November 1917. (Yakov Vladimirovich Steinberg)

A detachment of the Red Guard with a captured armoured car, an Austin II series. (Edward Alsworth,Ross)

The Putilov factory combat team at shooting practice, November 1917. (Yakov Vladimirovich Steinberg)

themselves who requisitioned the land and shared it out, preferring to keep the food than distributing it to the urban centres.

One of the first moves by the new Bolshevik government was to conclude an armistice with the Germans who had penetrated deep into Russian territory by this time. In February 1918 Trotsky led the peace delegation at Brest-Litovsk. Some wanted to continue a revolutionary war, the only alternative being a shameful peace. As part of the treaty Russia lost the Ukraine and other large areas of Russian territory to the Germans. Lenin believed that the Russian revolution would trigger a European revolution, yet even in Russia the revolution was not fully supported by the population. There were still many with leanings toward the old system and the Tsar. The civil war that was shortly to break out was instigated by nationalist army officers, right-wing politicians and the Church.

There had already been some dispute among the Cossacks. Their previous leader, General Kaledin, had given up command in favour of General Alexeieff who had organized an army of 30,000 men to fight the Bolsheviks. However a number of

"Russia First", a contemporary cartoon asking those with the torch of dissension to fight for Russia against the enemy of liberty.

younger Cossacks had become supporters of the Bolsheviks. There was also a threat from Polish legionaries.

The revolution had not been a uniform event across the Russian Empire and not everyone within the empire wanted to be part of the new Bolshevik Russia. After a meeting between the leaders of the Ukrainian movement of Russia and Galicia at Kiev the Ukraine was declared a republic and held elections to form a Ukrainian parliament. It was hoped that the Ukraine would be one of a series of republics within a Russian sphere of influence. The Bolsheviks saw otherwise and declared war, claiming to have captured Kiev.

The actions of the Ukrainian leaders were no doubt due to the belief that they would inherit large tracts of Russian and Polish territory from the Germans. Whether this was an intentional plan by the Germans to cause friction on the borders of the Ukraine seems likely. There had been a belief that Polish representatives would take part in the negotiations. In fact the Polish National Committee which was sitting in Paris stated that the land ceded to Ukraine in Poland was without the consent of the inhabitants: Poland wanted independence. The editor of the *Golos Polski*, published in Paris, Mr M. Rudnicki, said "I express the sentiment of all my compatriots without distinction of their party to say that the limits assigned to the Ukraine are irreconcilable with the historic rights of Poland."

However, some claimed that Poland had itself taken advantage of the standing down of the Russian forces to grab land for themselves. They had taken control of Mohileff adjoining Minsk, controlling the road to Moscow and the population that was mainly White Russians. If as seemed possible at this time that Russia was to dissolve into a number of smaller, independent states then each state could ostensibly introduce tariffs at its borders making German exports impossible.

The relationship between Russia and Britain was to change dramatically when the Bolsheviks came to power. While the Russians were still in the war, even if they were Bolsheviks, they were useful in bottling up several German armies on the Eastern Front. With the Treaty of Brest-Litovsk, that all changed with the British wary of the Bolshevik Russians—the Reds—and looking to support what would be known as the White Russians.

At the same time, there was the potential for the Russian revolution to foment social upheaval in the rest of Europe, even revolution, so much so that it even spread to the British army, where widespread sympathy for workers' movements led to several strikes by British troops in occupied Germany.

There was a belief much later that the Russian civil war was triggered by the uprising by Czech troops in May 1918. This was obviously not the case as fighting was evident in many areas much earlier than this. This would suggest that the revolution had been a peaceful event up until this time. It could also be argued that the civil war began with the revolution itself and the resulting fighting was between those with polarized ideologies of a future Russia which makes much more sense.

The Czech Legion had been formed in 1916 to fight for the Tsar against Germany and Austria. Many of the Legion were former Austro-Hungarian PoWs. After the revolution some were sent to fight for the Allies on the Western Front, but the Germans soon put a stop to this, pressurizing the new Russian government to disband the Legion, which in turn the Legion violently resisted and did play a large part in the conflict.

It wasn't only the Czechs that the Bolsheviks were fighting. What was known as the Railway War was to occur when train loads of revolutionary soldiers would travel to regions where there was no support for the revolution and forcibly put down any opposition. This was not possible everywhere and one of the revolution's earliest opponents were the Cossacks in southeast Russia, especially in the Don region. Resistance did not last long though and the Don force was defeated in early 1918, its remnants numbering around 4,000 fleeing onto the steppes to lick their wounds and regroup, and where it grew into a significant army by the end of 1918.

In the memoirs of Sergei Golitsyn, who came from a wealthy family who lost everything after the revolution, he remembered his cousin Vladimir Lvov who had been a cornet in the cavalry before the revolution but had remained loyal to old Russia. He owned a book showing the colourful uniforms of his regiment. He died fighting for the White Army. After driving the Reds out of a village where he had shot a commissar, the man, not dead, had shot Vladimir in the back as he walked away.

Members of the Czech Legion who many believed were responsible for starting the Russian Civil War.

One problem area for the Bolsheviks was Finland. Although there was early success for the revolution here, it did not last long. Finland was fiercely independent and even had its own parliament, the only regional government in the Russian Empire. The Whites in Finland might have been in the minority but they were aided by military advisers who had been trained in Germany. The Red Army in Finland was poorly trained and consisted mainly of local Finns sympathetic to the revolution but without any real support from Russia: in terms of Brest-Litovsk, the Russians had agreed to withdraw from Finland. With German support the Whites were able to defeat the Reds. The November 1918 collapse of the German army was to ultimately lead to Finnish independence.

Even though Russia was to lose the Baltic states—Estonia, Latvia and Lithuania—as well as Finland, the Ukraine and Belorussia, what was left of Russia was still enormous, its territory still eclipsing most of the Europe and its population still exceeding sixty million.

The uprising in the Volga basin in May 1918 was a serious threat to the Bolshevik government. The Czechs fighting in the area were joined by other forces opposed to the Bolsheviks and a rival government was proclaimed, the Komuch. The Red Army suffered from a paucity of troops on the ground and was not helped by a mutiny with its regional commander Muraviev switching sides and going over to the Czechs.

Nicholas II, his wife, their five children and all those who had followed them into imprisonment were murdered in mid-July 1918. This was carried out by Bolshevik troops but it was only Nicholas's death that was announced. It was later publicized that the others had also died at the hands of left-wing revolutionaries before it was then denied that they were dead at all. It was not officially confirmed that they were all dead until 1926 yet it was always denied by Lenin that the Bolshevik government had any part in the murders. The news sent shock waves through the previous elite, and through the monarchies of Europe. Golitsyn said that his family heard the news through a telegram from his mother in Moscow, that there had a very short mention of the executions in the newspapers. At this time the family was still living on their large estate. A mass was said for the Tsar at the church on the Golitsyn estate. Lenin claimed that no ethnic Russians were involved in the murder, that those responsible were Latvians and, of course, Jews.

Rumours of the Tsar's death had been circulating in the British press from early July. *The Times* claimed that Nicholas had been bayonetted by a soldier in an altercation on a train from Ekateringburg to Perm. It was claimed that when the royal family got off the train the Tsar was not with them. However, a further report, said to come from *Pravda*, stated that Nicholas was shot by soldiers at the riding school outside Ekaterinburg on 26 July, apparently to prevent him falling into the hands of counter-revolutionaries.

By the summer there was a danger of not only Bolshevik rule on the Volga collapsing but in the rest of Russia as well. Muraviev was then shot by a worker called Vareiikis who claimed that he had committed suicide. With their leader's death the uprising almost collapsed but fighting continued throughout the summer, only ending in the semblance of a Red victory as winter approached.

"The Liberators", a contemporary cartoon depicting the Bolsheviks as having destroyed the law, the economy, treaties and the armed forces in Russia.

The danger to the Bolsheviks from the Whites was not only in large-scale battle but in isolated attacks. In August 1918 Lenin was shot and seriously injured by a woman, Fanny Kaplan. The head of the Petrograd secret police was assassinated at the same time. The result of these attacks led to was what became known as the Red Terror. The aim of it was to exterminate the bourgeoisie.

In late summer a serious uprising in the southeast erupted where the Cossacks retook their capital Novocherkassk and bitter warfare broke out across the Don. During the Railway War the Reds had brutally put down any counter-revolutionary activity but in doing so had turned many against the revolution.

With German troops advancing into the Ukraine, support for the Whites came from Colonel Drozdovsky's and Denikin's volunteers in the south. The Cossacks themselves had wide military experience. They were led by General Petr Krasnov, a Cossack commander in the First World War. His cavalry corps had threatened Petrograd during the October revolution. Their uprising was helped by the Red forces having to fight on several fronts. The success on the Don led to the Cossack army moving west across the Don.

There is an argument to rival the Czech Legion theory that the civil war began when an independent Don republic was declared by General Kaledin and other Cossack communities in the Kuban and in Orenburg. At the same time, in Siberia, Grigori Semenov who was half-Cossack and half-Mongolian also rebelled. But the Cossacks were held up at the battle of Tsaritsyn. One of the defenders of the city was Joseph Stalin who was in sharp dispute with Trotsky's use of former Tsarist officers in the Red forces. (Stalin was from an impoverished Georgian family who had joined the Russian Social Democratic Party and edited their newspaper *Pravda*. He also enjoyed much success as a fundraiser for Lenin, often through crime.)

The lack of success of the Cossack army was due to the fact that promised support from other White factions did not materialize—a recurring factor in the failure of the Whites, with all the separate factions pursuing their own agendas. Denikin's volunteer army had moved to the Kuban region and it was this lack of cohesion in White forces that was to be prove their greatest weakness and eventual undoing, a reflection of the Russian armies during the First World War.

The Volunteer Army enjoyed a great deal of success in the Kuban. The Whites now had their own base on which they could build their own state. But helping the Cossacks was possibly counterproductive as the Cossacks had little interest in fighting outside of their own homelands, with no great desire to get involved in a wider conflict.

By mid-1918, the Whites were making progress elsewhere in the country The Soviets had lost the Urals and Siberia. Although this may have had a great deal to do with the Czech forces, it was also due to the fact that Soviet presence was thin on the ground. Most of the population were peasants working the land, with little sympathy or understanding of the workers' revolution.

There were also large numbers of ex-Tsarist officers in the non-Bolshevik regions with many thousands flocking to join the anti-Bolshevik alliance. Toward the end of 1918 Admiral Alexander Kolchak became the supreme head of the 'Provisional All-Russian Government' based in Omsk in southwestern Siberia and for almost two years he was internationally regarded as head of the White government, in spite of the fact that he was never able to unite the disparate White regions. (Kolchak came from a minor noble family in Petrograd whose father had been a major-general in the Marine Artillery. While serving in the navy Kolchak took part in the Russian polar expedition of 1900. He became the youngest vice-admiral in the Russian navy, in 1916. He was very reliant on Allied aid during his time in command of the White army which led to his being described as a western puppet. He stubbornly refused to consider autonomy for ethnic minorities and refused to cooperate with non-Bolshevik left-wing groups.)

After Denkin's army had taken the Kuban region, they pushed through in early 1919 in an attempt to take the Caucasus region, defeating the vastly numerically superior Soviet Eleventh Army in the process and capturing thousands of prisoners and hundreds of tons of material. The entire Caucasus then fell to Deniken with the collapse of the Soviet Twelfth Army

It wasn't only the Whites who lacked cohesion: there was constant in-fighting between Soviet leaders over the organization of the Red Army which also hindered operations. Many of the officers in the early days following the revolution were previous members of the Tsar's armies. In early 1919 Lenin was considering getting rid of these officers but eventually came round to Trotsky's way of thinking in keeping the officers in place as at least they had some military experience which many Bolsheviks did not. The success of this situation is still unclear. There were many occasions when Tsarist officers changed sides and went over to the Whites. In June there were attempts by such officers to open the gates of Petrograd to the Whites. The commander of the Ninth Army defected. Literally hundreds of officers were arrested in mid-1919 and shot.

In 1919, Western European nations began to get overtly involved in the civil war, often purely for their own interests. The French along with Greek and Senegalese troops occupied Odessa, wanting control of the Ukraine. They were defeated by the Red Army and eventually left. In April 1919 there was a mutiny on French naval vessels in Odessa which led to the evacuation of the port. There was obviously some sympathy for the new Russian dispensation among the French sailors. Many of them wanted to go home after the war and did not want to fight in a Russian war they did not understand nor have any interest in. The French incident was kept quiet for months afterward. In Britain Churchill refused to believe that the French had left. Churchill was one of the Bolsheviks' greatest opponents. There were still fears in Russia though that the Allies would interfere in the civil war and Lenin urged British communists to forge electoral agreements with the Labour Party to defeat Lloyd George. There is little doubt that there was a great deal of sympathy for the Bolsheviks among the British and European working classes.

Lenin though did seem to have little understanding of the situation in Europe. If he still believed that there was a possibility of revolution throughout the continent, he was sadly mistaken: the war had not brought capitalism to its knees as he had hoped.

The most likely White entity to succeed was the Siberian army of former Tsarist Admiral Kolchak, as mentioned. There were even attempts during the Paris peace conference to recognize Kolchak as the leader of the legitimate Russian government. Another White leader who enjoyed Allied support was Anton Denikin, a former Tsarist general who at one point controlled much of the south and overran the Ukraine. (Unlike most Russian officers Denikin came from a lowly family. His father was a serf who had spent twenty-five years in the Russian army and retired as a major. Denikin was born in what is now Wlocawek in Poland. As a young man he went to a military college and eventually rose through the ranks to become a Tsarist general.)

Winston Churchill, one of the Bolsheviks' main antagonists in Europe; he even sanctioned using chemical weapons against them.

In autumn 1919 Deniken was within 200 miles of Moscow, advancing from the south while General Mamontov's forces were also making progress against the Reds. In what would become trademark Bolshevik brutality, as the White armies approached a town, the Reds would take the towns' civil servants, merchants and landowners behind the lines and shoot them.

Reports of the seemingly unstoppable advances of the White armies were appearing in all the Western newspapers, as were accounts of peasant uprisings.

There were numerous uprisings in late 1919–early 1920, often violent reactions to the government food squads scouring the countryside.

There was also a drought in the summer of 1920 which led to even shorter supplies of food. It wasn't only peasants suffering: newspapers printed lists of those executed that often included notables from Moscow society.

Evidence of what was going on is shown in thousands of personal stories. The chaos in the administration of the country was highlighted by the fate of an uncle of Sergi Golitsyn, commander of a motorized cavalry company during the First World War. Hearing that his former commander, General Brusilov, was now one of Trotsky's deputies, he went to see him. Despite being a royalist he agreed to take a post in the Red Army as he had the safety of his family to think of. He was given papers authorizing him to travel to Orel to report to his new unit. He decided to visit his family in Bogoroditsk on the way. He was then arrested and despite his reasons for the minor diversion, instead of being sent to his unit, he was sent to prison.

The survival of the Bolshevik government was a close-run thing in the early days of the civil war. The Whites were making inroads as supplies to the Red Army dwindled dangerously. Factory workers did not help matters in that they were uninterested in the civil war. The result was 'War Communism', a system in which there were strict controls on workers and strikes were banned despite the strike being the main tool of the revolution.

A civilian car requisitioned by the Bolsheviks in the early days of the February revolution in Petrograd.

Famine had taken hold in Moscow and bread was rationed. Those who had possessions of any value travelled out into the countryside to barter for flour and potatoes. Often fine old paintings were exchanged for meagre amounts of food, which might then perversely be confiscated by officials. It was impossible to buy train tickets so people crowded into goods wagons. Armed government food squads roamed the countryside, requisitioning what food stocks they could find and paying for it in worthless Red roubles. It was not only the urban workers who had to be provided for during the civil war; the Red Army had to be fed too. The peasants suffered accordingly and a man-made famine swept the land. Lenin's secret police, the ubiquitous Cheka, sought out enemy agents, counter-revolutionaries and any enemy of the people, real or imagined. Harbouring food stocks was regarded as counter-revolutionary, a crime punishable by exile or death. Mass Bolshevik demonstrations and rallies took place across the country with red flags and banners bedecking town squares.

In April 1919 conscription was introduced, including the drafting of labour for what was seen as essential work. At the same time labour camps were also introduced for offenders. The most serious offenders—counter-revolutionaries—were sent to concentration camps, the nee gulags.

Toward the end of 1919 things were looking dire for the Soviets with White armies pressing from a number of points. Many Red Army soldiers deserted or changed sides. Despite this, the numbers involved were far smaller on the White side than in the Red Army: the northwestern White Army, for example, never numbered more than 15,000 men.

Denikin's army, however, did little to endear itself with the local populace during its advanced, due to the fact that his troops were responsible for innumerable atrocities, slaughtering literally thousands. There was also a strong anti-Jewish sentiment among Denikin's men and he allowed a number of pogroms to take place under his watch. Even Churchill warned him about his treatment of Jews.

The success of the Whites in late 1919 came to an abrupt halt. Denikin's army was on the verge of flooding into Moscow when they were stopped by the Reds and pushed back across the Don. The people had not forgotten the atrocities and supplies to the Whites dwindled. Their own early success with cavalry now told against them as the new, vastly improved Red cavalry was one of the principal causes for their defeat and despite a brief stand at the Don, the disparate groups in the White army— never at best a cohesive unit—soon folded.

At the same time Kolchak's army began to fail. While Denikin was making his last stand on the Don, Siberia was falling back into Soviet hands. The White force began to fall apart as men deserted in droves while many of those left behind were sick. The rivers of Siberia that had once been formidable obstacles to the Bolsheviks were now frozen, allowing the Red Army to advance easily enough into the region.

There was to be one last hurrah by the Whites, in early 1920 in the Crimea. This was under General Petr Nikolayevich Vrangel who had replaced Denikin. Vrangel came late to the fight against the Soviets. (Vrangel was born in Mukuliai, now part of Lithuania, into an ethnic German family. He had fought in both the Japanese War and the First World War as a cavalry officer and eventually ended up as a colonel of a Cossack regiment.) At the same time, in January 1920, Kolchak was captured and executed by firing squad, calmly meeting his end "like an Englishman".

However, this was not the end of the problems for the Bolsheviks as in April Pilsudski launched a Polish invasion of the Ukraine and occupied Kiev in May. He wanted what was a hotly contested Ukraine as a buffer state between Poland and Russia. His force consisted of many from the beaten White forces; it was also well supplied with weapons. The Reds had no way of attacking the Crimean Peninsula by sea as they had very few ships; most of the remaining navy was in White hands. Pilsudski's invasion was eventually halted in October 1920 and his army pushed back. A ceasefire was implemented before the Allies intervened to set the new borders. The war against Poland was also due in some measure to Lenin seeing Poland as spring-board for spreading communism to the rest of Europe; however Britain wanted an independent Poland as a barrier, along with Germany, against the Russians and France wanted a strong Poland as an ally against Germany in case of further belligerence.

In the meantime, the Whites had made some progress in taking more of the Crimea but the armistice between Russia and Poland in October left the Red Army free to concentrate its resources in the areas surrounding the Black Sea. Despite stiff resistance, the Reds finally took the Crimea with an army three times the size of the Whites. However Vrangel and many of his army escaped by sea. Those left behind did not fare as well and it is impossible to quantify those executed, suffice to say that numbers ran to the thousands.

Bolshevism was based on urban ide-ology: their policies in the countryside were unworkable. The success of the October revolution was in part due to the lack of an organized opposition and

'Strike the Bolshevik!' A 1920 Polish propaganda poster.

The Polish 5th Legion Infantry Regiment in Dyneburg (Latvia), January 1920, during the Polish-Soviet war. (Centralne Archiwum Wojskowe)

Polish commanders, Marshal Józef Piłsudski, General Paul Henrys and General Leonard Skierski, during the 1920 war with Russia. (Instytut Piłsudskiego w Ameryce)

what political Tsarist elite there was left had as good as disappeared by the end of 1919. By 1921 it was clearly evident that the country was still in desperate straits; a new economic policy was introduced to prevent the economy collapsing completely. Some private ownership was restored in the agricultural sector and in some small businesses. Many saw this as a betrayal of the revolution but shops reopened and food gradually became more available.

6. THE TERROR YEARS

The fact that serious violence took place in both the 1905 and the 1917 revolutions can come as no surprise. The Russian state was no stranger to inflicting violence on the subject races of her empire throughout history, whether Tsarist or Soviet. The police and army were just as likely, in any era, to carry out orders to fire on their own people.

There was a serious uprising in Poland in January 1863. According to *The Times* of 26 January, "The whole kingdom of Poland has been declared in a state of siege." On the night of the 22nd attacks were carried out on Russian soldiers, with the insurgents killing any soldiers they could find. Many were strangled in their beds in the houses where they were billeted. Once the Russian troops managed to regroup, the insurgents were repulsed and large numbers of prisoners were taken. Russian casualties included many high-ranking officers: Colonel Kiglianpow was killed and General Kanabich was wounded. Fighting spread to Warsaw, Plock, Pionsk Radzyn and Siedlec. It was the conscription of Poles into the Russian army that was the cause of the uprising. Conscription had been stopped in Poland but

Bloody Sunday, Petrograd.

A 1919 Japanese propaganda lithograph of the Japanese army coming ashore at Vladivostok. The Japanese were defeated by the Soviets and were forced to withdraw by 1922. (Library of Congress)

had been reinstated in early January. On 14 January police and soldiers had arrived at the houses of men to be conscripted. If they were not there their parents were taken instead as guarantees of their giving themselves up for service. Those found were locked inside the Citadel in Warsaw. It was reported that 500 men who had been conscripted had deserted. They fled to Austria where they were welcomed. In Warsaw another 2,000 conscripts deserted and joined the uprising, with hostages taken by the Russian troops in their place.

The Times of 9 February commented on the acts that had inspired the uprising by the Poles. The report stated that "it was amazing that such atrocities can be committed in our day by a responsible and legal authority in the heart of Europe." It wasn't conscription as such that *The Times* was so against but how it was carried out. The report went on to describe it as "downright kidnapping". There was though, according to *The Times*, more to it than a simple attempt to swell the ranks of the Russian army: it was to drain the lifeblood of the Polish people by decimating the class of men—a generation in fact—who would become the country's leaders.

Conscription was not the only problem facing Poland: anti-Jewish pogroms, like those in Russia, burgeoned. Violence against Jews was encouraged in the Russian press. One of the worst of these was the newspaper *Bessarabetz*, published by Pavel Krushevan in Kishinev, capital of Bessarabia. which in the early 20th century printed banner headlines such as "DEATH TO THE JEWS" and "CRUSADE AGAINST THE HATED RACE", going so far as to claim that a boy who had died of natural causes in Dubossary and a girl who had committed suicide had in actuality been murdered by Jews who used their blood for a religious ceremony. On 19 April, Easter 1903, as congregations were leaving their churches, rioting 'sporadically' broke out. Forty-seven Jews were killed, ninety-two severely wounded and 500 injured. Hundreds of Jewish women were raped, 700 houses destroyed and 600 shops pillaged. *The Times* published a dispatch from Plehve, the minister of the interior, to the governor of Bessarabia that supposedly gave orders not to stop the rioters which apparently proved that the government supported the killings. This was believed to be a forgery but there was still no effort to prevent the attacks on the Jews. According to the *New York Times* of 28 April 1903,

> The mob was led by priests and the general cry was kill the Jews. They were taken wholly unaware and were slaughtered like sheep. The dead number 120 and the scenes of horror attending this massacre are beyond description. Babes were literally torn to pieces by the frenzied and bloodthirsty mob. At sunset the streets were piled with corpses.

The Russian ambassador to the United States, Count Arthur Cassini, was to say of the pogrom:

> The situation in Russia, so far as the Jews are concerned, is just this: It is the peasant against the money lender, and not the Russians against the Jews. There is no feeling against the Jew in Russia because of religion. It is as I have said—the Jew ruins the peasants, with the result that conflicts occur when the latter have lost all their worldly possessions and have nothing to live upon. There are many good Jews in Russia, and they are respected. Jewish genius is appreciated in Russia, and the Jewish artist honoured. Jews also appear in the financial world in Russia. The Russian Government affords the same protection to the Jews that it does to any other of its citizens, and when a riot occurs and Jews are attacked the officials immediately take steps to apprehend those who began the riot, and visit severe punishment upon them.

Between 1791 and 1835 Russia had acquired territory that was home to large numbers of Jews. The first pogroms of the 19th century are believed to have begun in 1821 in Odessa when the Greek Orthodox Patriarch Gregory V was executed in Constantinople. Greek residents blamed the Jews and fourteen were killed.

Russian workers became targets in early 20th-century Russia. When Father Gapon led a workers' rally to the Winter Palace in January 1905 the march was fired upon and attacked by the army and police. Although the events of Bloody Sunday are often portrayed as a battle in front of the Winter Palace, it was more of a series of clashes at bridges, gates and other entry points to the inner city. According to one report the group led by Father Gapon was fired on at the Narva Gate and forty people were killed. According to Gapon's version the group was attacked by Cossacks who used swords on men, women and children and over a hundred died. At 2 p.m. the Nevesky Prospekt was crowded with families as was normal for a Sunday afternoon. There were some workers among them making their way to join the march but many were innocent families out for a stroll. A detachment of guards arrived and formed two columns before opening fire on the innocent crowd. There were differing reports of how many were killed and injured on Bloody Sunday. Government figures were ninety-six dead and 333 injured. Anti-government sources claimed 4,000 dead. The true figure is no doubt somewhere between the two figures.

The workers on the streets were one of the main problems that the Tsar had to deal with and he did so with extreme levels of violence. But the shocking events of June 1905 must have made even the thick-skinned Tsar sit up and take notice: the Black Sea Fleet mutinied.

The best remembered of the ships was the battleship *Potemkin* but the mutiny also involved a transport ship and two torpedo boats. The ships had left Sevastopol for Odessa and the crews mutinied after an officer shot an insubordinate seaman. Violence by officers against the lower ranks was common in the Russian armed forces but shooting one of their own men was extreme. The trouble began after the crew complained that their ration meat was full of maggots. The ship's doctor disagreed and said it was fit to eat. When the crew complained to the ship's captain one of his officers lost his temper and shot one of the complainants. The offending officer was then shot and thrown overboard. The crews then revolted and drowned most of the officers with the exception of those needed to navigate the ships. When they reached Odessa the mutineers fired on the boats sent to demand their surrender. Four warships were then deployed with instructions to sink the mutinous ships but only two of them sailed as the crews on the other two were not thought to be trustworthy.

At the same time, unrest ashore in Odessa had broken out with large numbers of strikes and riots taking place. When troops were sent to deal with the crowds the rebel seamen shelled them, killing a number of Cossacks. The docks were on fire with foreign ships in danger while the mob stopped any attempts to put out the fires. The death toll rapidly mounted, topping two thousand. Martial law was declared as the army began firing indiscriminately into the crowds. The remaining officers from the

Potemkin were sent ashore with a demand that the seaman who had been shot be buried with full naval honours. Thousands followed the coffin to the naval cemetery.

The Tsar then reacted by declaring war in, or on, Odessa. It is hard to understand how declaring war on your own people might be a way to guarantee public safety which he claimed was the reason for the declaration. The commander of the troops now had the special rights of civil administration for the defence of order. As they had already been shooting protestors this can't have made much difference. There were still doubts as to whether the troops would join the mutineers. *The Times* of 4 July reported that the death toll now stood at 6,000 but that as to the situation, "How grave it is is hard to say, partly because it is misleading to interpret them by European standards." Did the rest of Europe believe that the actions of the Russian government were in some way uncivilized and not how other European governments would behave? (*The Times* clearly thought so, "that in a more highly organized society with a greater political and social life the events in Russia would be seen as tokens of impending dissolution of the government. There are obviously portions of the Russian armed forces that could no longer be trusted.") The *Potemkin* had by this time left Odessa and sailed to Constanza in Romania where the crew applied for asylum. The ships that had been sent to deal with the mutiny did not fire on the other ships that had remained in Odessa. The Tsar asked the Romanian government to treat the crew of the *Potemkin* as criminals. The ship was eventually returned to Russian control.

The problems began again in Russia in early February 1917 when fifteen workmen were arrested including eleven members of the Central Industrial Munitions Committee on a charge of revolutionary conspiracy. Alexander Protopopov, the minister of the interior, believed that all public bodies in Russia were animated by revolutionary conspiracy. However, when crowds gathered on the streets of Petrograd in March it was not due to revolutionary aims but worries about survival. There had been heavy snow and the transport of food to the city had been delayed. The citizenry was panicking that bread would run out and there were attacks on the supply chain. The authorities reacted in the normal way and General Sergey Khabalov, Petrograd's military commander, banned all public assemblies, warning the population that the troops had been ordered to use force to preserve order. Labour unrest in Russia had not hitherto assumed dangerous forms and had not prejudiced munitions production in spite of the wholesale transfer of workers to the front as a measure to curtail labour dissent. However, repression backfired in other areas. Government action against the Zemstov Unions had seriously affected the distribution of food supplies.

However, by the autumn, despite the Tsar's abdication and a new government being formed, the situation was getting progressively worse. In October there was rioting at Kharkov that, according to the Russian press, was due to "dark forces". In Astrakhan stores were set on fire. Peasants from Kaluga arrived at Kursk to buy corn, despite this being against regulations. They were supported in this by a train full of soldiers. Peasants in places such as Mogilev and Saratov were taking over estate lands, cattle and even manor houses. Tashkent had no contact with the capital whatsoever with a self-appointed government in place until a military force was sent from Samara to regain control. In Petrograd there was a serious increase in crime with robberies being carried out on the streets in broad daylight.

The American attitude to the revolution was seemingly favourable in its earlier days. When Woodrow Wilson addressed Congress in January 1918 he welcomed Russia "into the society of free nations". It seems though that Wilson only supported the revolution because he expected Russia to turn to democracy, but later described Bolshevism as "the poison of disorder and revolt". Eventually American troops would be sent to Russian to assist the Whites in their struggle against the Red Army.

Shortly after the revolution the British and French were considering the idea of sending troops to Vladivostok to prevent the new government from taking control of military supplies provided by the Allies. This included the idea of using Japanese or even American troops to achieve this. In fact the Russian press was already claiming by early 1918 that the Americans were supporting anti-Bolshevik forces in the south. The Americans were in fact at this time funnelling financial support through the British and the French rather than taking an active part themselves.

American troops march through Vladivostok.

Despite seeming to have no part in the support for the Whites, there is little doubt that the Americans were aggressively gathering intelligence, even increasing the number of consuls in the country. Of course Britain had been using writers as agents for some time in Russia. As mentioned, one famous foreign name in Russian politics in the early days of the revolution was Somerset Maugham. He had been given the task of keeping the Russians in the war and in keeping Kerensky in power. There seemed to have been little secrecy in the early role of the spy. Maugham is supposed to have said to the partner of the writer John Reed, Louise Bryant, "You won't say that you had lunch with a British secret agent will you?" There appeared to be a certain regard for the use of writers as agents by the British in Russia and elsewhere: it was thought that their powers of observation made them very useful. Maugham had been offered the chance to spy for Britain by John Wallinger, a senior officer in the Secret Service Bureau. Wallinger was already running teams of agents in Germany and Switzerland. Maugham had an ideal cover as a writer, retiring to a neutral country to write in peace. He moved to Switzerland in late 1915. His main duties were in passing on information gathered by agents in Germany under the codename of Somerville. He returned home in May 1916 in very poor health. He was later recruited to work in Russia, arriving in Petrograd in August 1917. He found the city in a sorry state. He said that since the February revolution there had been a feeling of uncertainty with riots and gunfire on the streets, exacerbated by crowds of soldiers who had deserted from the front. Despite the situation and the lack of food, the trams still ran, shops and restaurants were still open and the cinemas were showing films starring Charlie Chaplin and Douglas Fairbanks.

The British embassy had been informed that Maugham was in Russia on a special mission but he reported that his first meeting with the British ambassador, Sir George Buchanan, did not go well. He described the ambassador as a cardboard cutout of a typical ambassador whose reception of Maugham was distinctly chilly; Maugham realized that he would receive little support from the embassy. He managed to get himself introduced to Kerensky but found him to be a sick man who had lost his vision. He constantly changed his mind and seemed very nervous. Maugham almost instantly decided that he was not worthy of Allied support.

At this time Kerensky was being pressured by the Allies to continue with the war against Germany while the Russian population, facing famine, was calling for an end to the fighting. Yet despite the Allied pressure on the prime minister, the Allied ambassadors in Russia were offering very little in the way of material support. It seems that Maugham was unsuccessful in both his tasks when the second revolution of 1917 saw the Bolsheviks come to power. He had not believed that there was much hope for Kerensky's government and that the Bolsheviks were bound to eventually take power. He did however enjoy the experience of discovering Russia.

When it became clear that the Bolsheviks were soon to assume power, in October, it was decided to recall Maugham who it was felt would be in some danger. Kerensky asked Maugham to deliver a message to the British prime minister, Lloyd George, asking him to offer Germany peace terms that they were bound to refuse. This would then, Kerensky believe, inspire the Russian army to carry on fighting. Lloyd George refused. It was after the revolution that the role of a British spy in Russia became considerably more dangerous. Many took on new identities and took to wearing disguise; messages were sent in invisible ink through teams of mules.

The Times of 3 November described some of the events in Petrograd. Two men and a woman were seen trying to steal cloth from a shop and were arrested by the militia. By this time a large crowd had gathered. The crowd rushed the shop and forcibly abducted the thieves from the militia. One of the male thieves was shot dead by someone in the crowd while the other was badly beaten before being taken to hospital. The crowd then returned for the woman who was also shot dead. In another incident two men were walking down a street firing pistols. They were then attacked by a crowd who beat them senseless before they were taken to hospital. The report went on to say that the anarchical wave in the country was spreading and that martial law was being declared in an increasing number of towns.

There was serious fighting in Petrograd in mid-November after military cadets loyal to the government occupied the telephone exchange. What were described as extremist supporters then attempted to retake it. When called on to surrender the cadets refused as they claimed to be acting under orders. Fighting then broke out at four cadet schools. At the Vladimir School there were prolonged clashes with the revolutionary forces using field guns against the cadets. When the Red Guard finally took the school a number of the cadets were killed. The school building was also seriously damaged. The bodies of the young cadets were then thrown into the street.

The Winter Palace was bombarded by the cruiser *Aurora* and was also fired upon from the St Peter and Paul fortress on the opposite bank of the Neva. Red Guards used machine guns and armoured cars to assault the cadets and women's battalion inside the palace.

In the early morning hours of 7 November Red Guards tried to take control of Petrograd's biggest newspaper, but finding the offices strongly guarded by armed men, they failed. At one o'clock in the morning, armed revolutionary soldiers and sailors from the Kronstadt naval base took over the city's telegraph exchange then occupied the post office and the telephone exchange. At dawn, a Bolshevik force surrounded the state bank before armed revolutionaries surrounded the Winter Palace, which held the offices of the provisional government.

One of the most important events in relation to Britain was Lenin's cancellation the Anglo-Russian Convention of 1907 that outlined spheres of influence of both Russia and Britain in Central Asia and protected India's northern borders from Russian aggression. Lenin went further than just cancellation: he urged Asia's oppressed populations to throw off the yoke of colonial rule. The obvious reaction to this aggression on the part of the Russian government would be for the British to take military action against Lenin. This was considered but with a war against Germany to win, Britain did not have the available manpower.

At around this time another man was about to become involved in the British espionage ring in Russia. Sidney Reilly had been an arms dealer in the U.S., sending weapons to the Russians. He was a brilliant linguist who could take on another identity in an instant and was able to pass as both a Russian and a German. But he was a loose cannon who did not follow orders easily. He disembarked at Murmansk instead of Archangel but the port was being guarded by British marines, sent there to prevent Allied munitions falling into German hands. The marines arrested Reilly believing that he was a revolutionary.

He was able to prove who he was to another British agent, Stephen Alley, by showing a message written in a code that Alley recognized. Alley was on his way home after being sacked for what he claimed was his refusal to assassinate Stalin. If true then it seems that Britain was trying to take a far more active role in the fight against the Bolsheviks. Reilly loathed the Bolsheviks and urged Britain to land a large

British Marines and the Naval Brigade march through Batum, on the Georgian Black Sea coast.

military force to help the marines already there to protect allied stores in Russian ports. He also wanted Britain to support opposition groups in Russia that he hoped would eventually topple Lenin's government.

There seemed to be little control of the revolutionary forces in the early days as one of the commissars attacking the military cadets tried to stop the killing of the young cadets. The attackers then turned on him and his own life was only saved by the arrival of members of another committee. The uncertain situation in Petrograd was causing problems in many areas. When *The Times* correspondent tried to send a cablegram in mid-November he found that the staff of the post office and telegraph office were refusing to work because of the uncertainty of their wages. When a telegram did reach London from the British ambassador Sir George Buchanan it stated that all was quiet in Petrograd but that Kerensky, accompanied by General Alexeieff, was approaching the city with a large force of Cossacks; he further stated that the city was under control of the Bolsheviks but that the Bolshevik troops had no officers.

There were rumours circulating of fierce fighting in Gatchina, Pulkova and Tsarakoe Selo, all of which were close to Petrograd. The Military Revolutionary Committee was claiming that Kerensky had been defeated. However, Kerensky had three Cossack regiments, a school of military cadets and squadrons of armoured cars in the areas mentioned. Opposing him were the Petrograd garrison and a large number of guards. The ensuing clash took place at Pulkova, only six miles from Petrograd. The battle lasted three days before the Red Guards eventually drove back the Cossacks, the Cossack cavalry being decimated by armoured car machine-gun fire. A large number of civilians died during the fighting, setting the tone for the next few months.

Kerensky had been hoping for support from the soldiers fighting at the front but it quickly became evident that this was not going to happen. The Cossacks supporting him were becoming disillusioned. After being approached by members of the extremists, the Cossacks decided to stop fighting and arrest Kerensky who had promised to go to Petrograd and face the Military Revolutionary Committee but had then, wisely, changed his mind and fled.

The defeat of Kerensky did seem to have an effect on the situation in Petrograd as trams were running again and life was beginning to get back to some kind of order. Banks and even theatres were reopening though bread was still in short supply.

The same could not be said of other parts of the country. In Moscow the Military Revolutionary Committee had organized an uprising against the Committee of Public Safety. Most of the garrison and the Red Guards supported the revolutionaries. The White Guards and military cadets supported the Public Safety Committee. The extremists were driven from the Kremlin by the cadets after a fierce fight. The extremists then put it under siege using field guns. They also attacked the Hotel Metropole where a number of foreigners were staying. They were rescued by

The Cossacks were loyal to the Tsar prior to the revolution. Many sided with the Whites against the Bolsheviks during the civil war.

foreign consuls. During the attack on the Kremlin art treasures sent from Petrograd for safety were destroyed. The fighting went on for several days with between 8,000 and 10,000 deaths. Eventually an armistice was arranged, prisoners on both sides were exchanged and the Public Safety Committee was disbanded before the Military Revolutionary Committee took control of the city. Meanwhile negotiations continued between the extremists and more moderate socialist groups.

The revolts in the army and the navy after the revolution led to the massacre of many of the officers. According to the Allies these acts were encouraged by the Germans—General Nogin was killed for a reward of £1,500 stumped up by the Germans—but in many cases there seemed little if any encouragement needed. At Helsingfors in Finland, for example, well back from the front, troops seized forty officers. Generals Vasilieff and Aronovsky, Colonel Karemius and seven other high-ranking officers were thrown off a bridge and shot at as they tried to swim away. When Colonel Karemius climbed out of the water his head was smashed in, another officer was beheaded and Colonel Djunin was lynched.

After a mutiny aboard some Russian ships, officers were supposedly burned at the stake while others were thrown through holes in the ice in frozen waters. This was again according to *The Great War* magazine and again it seems that there may have been some level of exaggeration as one of the admirals listed as being executed in

Another contemporary cartoon, this one depicting Anarchy—Russian revolutionaries—
being bought off with German gold to turn against the Allies.

this way was Admiral Viren who was in fact killed but by bayonet. According to the
magazine one officer was even sawn in half.

It was understandable that the Allies, alarmed at Russia's withdrawal from the
war, were looking for any group within the country that might offer some resistance
against Germany before the war ended. There were a number of these. Trotsky accused

Lloyd George of scattering roulette chips on every number. Britain and France split Russia up into areas in which they would operate. Britain took the Caucasus, and France the Ukraine, Crimea and Bessarabia. Their ambassadors later withdrew to the north leaving some representatives to deal with a government they did not recognize.

When Sidney Reilly arrived in Petrograd in early 1918 he was unprepared for the changes that had taken place. He described it as having a ruinous and tumbledown aspect. The streets were dirty and neglected and many of the buildings were little more than ruins. The only police present were the secret police. There were no shops open and hardly any traffic on the roads. A state of panic existed, the rabble had been riotous and there had been widespread looting. Now there was nothing left to loot. The blood lust and destruction practised by the mobs had changed: they were now cowed and frightened. They were also starving—unlike the Bolsheviks.

As mentioned there was one foreign group that was to have a major influence in Russia. In May 1918 fighting erupted between Soviet forces and Czech troops in western Siberia where the Czechs took large swathes of the countryside including many major towns. The Czech force—based in the Ukraine but moved to Siberia in early 1918—had originated from workers who had immigrated to Russia in 1914.

The Soviets claimed that the outbreak of violence by the Czechs was due to the Allies who had encouraged them. There is some doubt about this as the French wanted the Czechs to fight on the Western Front while the British wanted them to prop up a new Eastern Front; thus their attack on the Bolshevik government did not really suit the Allies at that time. The real reason may have been attempts by the Bolsheviks to disarm the Czechs after a clash with Hungarian PoWs at Chelyabinsk. They then tried to have them transferred to the Russian army but in typical Bolshevik fashion then gave orders that any armed Czech was to be shot.

There was little doubt that the Allies did eventually see the Czechs as an advantage in their fight against the Soviet government but this seems to have occurred after the outbreak of fighting. Czech control in western Siberia meant that there was little chance of the Bolsheviks preventing any Allied landings in the ports of Murmansk and Archangel where there were large amounts of military stores.

The areas around the ports were sparsely populated compared with the industrial centres of Russia. There was little support for the Bolshevik government locally and the anti-Soviet movement grew after the Allies did in fact land there. In September 1918 a military coup took place, suspected of being instigated by the British.

The different agents working in Russia had their own views of who was the best person to support against the Bolsheviks. Some thought that the former minister of war, Boris Savinkov, was the best bet. (This was surprising considering his background. Although he had been part of the provisional government, he was a revolutionary himself having been expelled from university for taking part in student riots.

Members of the Czech
Legion along with one of
Russia's Asiatic citizens.

He had also been arrested for his part in the assassination of Grand Duke Sergei
Alexandrovich in 1906. He had been sentenced to death but escaped before the sentence was carried out.) His plan was to kill all the Bolshevik leaders when Allied
troops arrived in Murmansk and Archangel and to then form a new government.
Savinkov made his attempt in July 1918 despite the fact that no Allied troops had
arrived by then. The revolt was crushed by Latvian mercenaries led by Trotsky. It was
suspected that the revolt had been financed by the British and the French and restrictions were placed on the freedom movement of some Allied officers still in Russia.

This was to result in some of the agents who had been working openly in Russia
to go underground. Many of them took on new identities and disappeared from the
view of the Bolshevik secret police. One of those still operating overtly was Bruce

Lockhart, one of the first westerners to learn of the murder of the Tsar and his family and who sent the information to London.

Other Allied troops had also arrived in Russia by this time to follow the Japanese troops and British marines that had been landed in Vladivostok in April. Four foreign warships—one British, one American and two Japanese—invested the port, which had stopped the Bolsheviks from taking the city but they were still harassing foreigners. The number of Red Guards arriving in the city was rising daily: a Japanese shop in the city was robbed by Russian soldiers and three shop workers were shot. When the British marines were landed, there were only fifty of them; Moscow believed that a full-scale Allied invasion had begun. In fact the marines quickly returned to their ship. It was however the Czechs who ended Bolshevik control of the city in July. British troops then occupied Baku where the Bolsheviks had also been overthrown.

More Allied troops arrived in Archangel in August and in Moscow there were rumours that numbers were around 100,000. As a result hundreds of Allied nationals were arrested and held hostage by the Cheka. Some British agents managed to escape the net while living under assumed identities. The Allied encroachment into the country led to distrust of the Allies by the Bolsheviks and, after the attempt on Lenin's life in August, this led to further arrests and attacks on Allied citizens. There is little doubt that in most cases the Allies were sympathetic to the White forces. The senior British officer in Siberia, General Knox, was friends with Admiral Kolchak. (The French believed that it was the British who had helped to establish the admiral after the coup.)

British Royal Marines and the Durhams at Batum, Georgia.

In August Lockhart was contacted by a man who had been an important ally to the Bolsheviks: Berzin was a colonel in the Latvian mercenaries supporting the Bolsheviks. He told Lockhart that the Latvians had lost all confidence in the Bolsheviks and were worried at the prospect of having to face Allied troops on the battlefield. The Latvians wanted to return home to Latvia. Trying to turn the situation to their advantage, it was suggested that this would be easier to achieve if the Latvians helped topple the Bolshevik government. The plan, mainly organized by Reilly, was for the Latvians to assassinate Lenin and Trotsky at a particular meeting. The plan failed, betrayed before it could be put into operation.

There was, as mentioned, the attempt on Lenin's life in August when a young Socialist, Fanya (Fanny) Kaplan, shot him twice, just missing his heart. There were immediate reprisals and one of those arrested was Lockhart. It was obvious that Reilly's planned coup was common knowledge as Lockhart was grilled extensively about it. There was even some doubt as to whether Lockhart may have had something to do with the attempt on Lenin's life by Kaplan. The Bolsheviks claimed that he had been arrested because members of the Archangel Soviet had been shot at and Archangel was occupied by Allied forces.

Bolshevik antagonism manifested itself with an attack on the British mission in Moscow which led to several deaths, something abhorred by the British as "a gross outrage against civilzed people". When the Cheka attacked the British embassy in Petrograd, the Americans were led to belive that a state of war existed between the

British Royal Navy Captain Francis Newton Cromie (1882–1918).

Allies and the Bolsheviks. Although a number of Russians were killed in the attack, Captain Francis Cromie, chief of British intelligence in northern Russia, was also shot dead, apparently executed. Red Guards then threatened to shoot five of the embassy staff while at the same time some 500 of the old guard—writers, businessmen, civic leaders, clergy, intelligentsia—were rounded up and routinely executed.

The leader of the Cheka at the time of the Red Terror was Felix Dezerzhinsky who had at one time planned to become a priest. He came from an aristocratic family but turned to Marxism as he grew up. Arrested as a revolutionary, he was imprisoned for four years under the Tsar and only released after the revolution. He was appointed head of the Cheka by Lenin.

Lenin believed that extreme methods were needed to retain power. He had been furious when he found out that capital punishment had been ended for desertion in the Russian army. He saw the lack of a will to kill as a weakness. It was believed that many of those who were victims of the Red Terror were counter-revolutionaries: many were in fact just members of the wrong class. In an interview for the Bolshevik newspaper *Noyaya Zhizn*, Dezerhinsky admitted that he stood for organized terror, that it was an absolute necessity during times of revolution. Those arrested were judged quickly. Most were executed within twenty-four hours of their arrest. There were obviously no trials involved. Many of the victims were said to have confessed but this was no doubt due to torture in the interrogation process. The population were so scared that many would not pass the building where the Cheka were situated.

Lenin expounded that a ruthless reign of terror against the *kulaks* (peasants deemed more affluent), priests, White guards and Mensheviks was necessary but also added that all suspicious persons should be detained in concentration camps. He also wanted to get rid of prostitutes who got soldiers drunk. The list of those at danger also included. The attempt on Lenin's life may have come close to seriously damaging the revolution but the result was in fact a greater emphasis on the terror. The Bolshevik newspaper *Krasnaya Gazeta* said after the attempt on Lenin that "We will turn our hearts into steel in the fire of blood and suffering and the blood of fighters for freedom." It went on to say that they "would not quiver at the sight of a sea of enemy blood, we will kill our enemies in scores of hundreds".

Cheka arrests were made in the dead of night and the families of the arrested heard no more of them for some time, if at all. The Red Terror was no secret and was widely reported in the European press. Even in Germany there seemed to be revulsion. The *Berliner Lokal-Anzeiger* said, "One breathes with difficulty in Russia. A new wave of blood has spread from Moscow over the whole empire and threatens universal suffocation. The Bolshevik leaders assert that the Red Terror purifies the atmosphere like a thunderstorm and that the Soviet republic will stand mighty, strong and peaceful after it." The report went on to say that the Bolsheviks argued that the few thousand to suffer in the terror was nothing compared to the millions that the war remorselessly offered as a sacrifice to capitalism. But the cold-blooded striking down of defenceless persons and the nightly executions were likened to the events of the French Revolution. A squad of Russian soldiers was said to be kept in readiness to receive the victims on an arc-lit Petrograd square. One neutral diplomat stated: "The terror is growing worse and becoming more insensate daily."

In April 1919, during a speech at the Connaught Rooms in London, Churchill openly criticized Lenin and demanded Allied intervention in Russia. However, even the British press was strongly against any kind of Allied intervention, calling it

Churchill's private war. What Churchill did do was to arrange to send chemical weapons to the White forces in Russia along with other military supplies. British scientist had developed a top-secret weapon known as the M Device, a gas shell that released an arsenic-based gas, a dense smoke that would incapacitate anyone who breathed it in. It had originally been planned for use against the Germans. The stockpile of the weapon left over after the end of the war was shipped to Russia. Britain's imperial general staff knew there would be outrage if it became known that the government was intending to use its secret stockpile of chemical weapons against the Bolsheviks but Winston Churchill, then secretary of state for war, brushed aside concerns. As a long-term advocate of chemical warfare, he was determined to use the weapons against the Russian Bolsheviks in the summer of 1919, in spite of some disquiet in the British government. (Churchill also wanted to use it against the tribes of northern India who had been encouraged to rebel by the Bolsheviks, even arguing that the gas was more humane than high-explosive shells.) British aircraft began to drop the gas in late August 1919, south of Archangel, continuing into September. The dropping of the gas was followed by attacks by White Russians wearing gas masks, often supported by British troops. (There seems to be a belief that British troops did not actually fight in the Russian civil war but then how did more than 300 of them die?) The chemical attacks were not a success and the remaining shells were dumped in the sea rather than being returned to Britain.

Although there had been numerous cases of large-scale killings, often of innocent people, during the years of revolution, it was during the civil war that the worst atrocities took place. One of the most notorious examples of the slaughter of those supposedly opposed to the government was known as the Red Terror. According to some sources it lasted for a month, from September to October 1919. Others describe it as a period of brutal repression by the Bolsheviks lasting for the entire course of the civil war (and beyond). However one looks at it, the Red Terror was a period of mass killing carried out by the Bolsheviks, mainly by the Cheka, the secret police. Victims were normally former members of the Tsarist regime, former officers and members of the middle classes. The Terror began as a reprisal for the attempted assassination of Lenin by Fanny Kaplan and the assassination of the leader of the Petrograd Cheka, Moissei Uritsky, although Lenin had already ordered the introduction of mass terror some time before the assassination efforts.

There is a belief that the Bolsheviks had to use terror to retain power because they had little support among the population, their power base being among workers and soldiers. There is some truth in this as they had little support among the peasants as highlighted in the elections after the October revolution where they only managed to win a quarter of the votes.

Reprisals were swift: 500 members of the previous Tsarist regime were immediately executed after the assassination of the Cheka leader. Anyone who dared spread the faintest rumour against the Bolsheviks was sent to a concentration camp. In Petrograd alone 800 were executed and more than 6,000 imprisoned. In the first two months of the Terror between 10,000 and 15,000 were executed. The numbers of executions were recorded for each area, with between 2,000 to 3,000 killings as an apparent average in most towns. After the defeat of White general Pyotr Nikolayevich Vrangel in the Crimea in late 1920, the Reds offered of amnesty to the defeated White army. Thousands of those who surrendered were then executed. It wasn't only the Whites who suffered during the Red Terror. Thousands of men deserted from the Red Army during the course of the civil war. Some of the families of the deserters were taken hostage or killed in reprisal. Many of those captured were then executed which again numbered in the thousands.

Although the strike had been one of the more effective weapons of the workers against the Tsar's government, it soon became clear that it was no longer a wise course of action to be taken after the revolution. In Astrakhan strikers and Red Army soldiers who had supported them were taken in barges and thrown into the Volga with rocks tied round their necks: thousands died. The various modes of execution were no doubt implemented to add to the terror—*pour encourager les autres*. Men were tied to planks and fed into furnaces or boiling water. Scalping was common as was the flaying of skin. Rolling captives in barrels studded with nails was popular as were crucifixions and stonings. Some captives were bound, then positioned in a frozen street where water was poured over them before being allowed to freeze. Rats were placed in tubes bunged at one end and placed against a captive's body at the open end; the tube was then heated so that the terrified rat ate its way free through the body.

The clergy was a popular target: priests, monks and nuns were crucified, thrown into boiling tar, given communion of molten lead or drowned in holes through the ice of frozen lakes. The Terror also became a way to settle old scores and a useful tool for profiteers. Men were arrested so that their wives could buy their freedom with their bodies. Victims were stripped naked and their clothes and possessions stolen by their executioners. They were either machine-gunned in large batches or shot one by one in the back of the head, executed in cellars where the bodies would stack up. There is a belief that violence is a natural, intrinsic part of Marxism. Lenin saw human life as expendable in the cause of revolution. Marx in his writing believed that in some cases the old world had to perish to make way for the new. It could also be argued that human life in Russia had always been expendable whoever was in power.

It wasn't only the British army that played a part in the civil war: their navy did too. A British fleet had been resident in the Baltic off Estonia and Latvia since

Above: Anton Deniken.

Left: General Kornilov.

January 1919, with Admiral Sir Walter Cowan commanding. During the bombardment ordered by Trotsky of the Russian garrison of Kronstadt that had mutinied, a British torpedo boat commanded by Augustus Agar torpedoed the armoured cruiser *Oleg*. The attack was criticized back in Whitehall but praised by Cowan. Cowan also ordered an attack on the Russian fleet in the Gulf of Finland in which several Russian ships were sunk or badly damaged. Despite the dismay in some quarters over the attacks on Russian shipping—Britain was not formally at war with Russia—Agar was awarded a Victoria Cross. Allied troops in Russia were often caught in an invidious situation as official policy was often at odds with reality on the ground and the British government had no strategic aims, no clear-sighted goals, in the country.

The Red Terror may have been criticized by the Allies but the men they were supporting on the White side were not adverse to the use of terror themselves. Lavr Kornilov led an army of Whites during the Ice March in southern Russia in February 1918. The Ice March, also known as the First Kuban campaign, was a defining event of the civil war, the beginning of the end for the Whites. When the Red Army entered Rostov in February 1918, the White army retreated towards Kuban across the frozen steppes, hoping to garner the support of the Don Cossacks. The march went on for several weeks, almost annihilating Kornilov's forces, until 10 April when he was forced to attack the Red Army—with disastrous results. He had ordered his men to take no prisoners, telling them that the greater the terror the greater their victories. If needs be, he said, he would set fire to half the country and shed the blood of three-fourths of all Russians. Kornilov's army was taken over by Denikin after Kornilov's death. Both Kornilov and Denikin unleashed a reign of terror against the Jews, convenient targets for whoever was in a position of power at the time. In the town of Fastov, one tiny example, Denikin's army murderd more than 1,500 Jews, mainly women, children and the elderly. Between 100,000 and 150,000 Jews were murdered by White forces in Ukraine and southern Russia.

In the Don Province the Soviet government was overthrown by the Whites in early 1918. More than 45,000 people were shot or hanged until the Red Army returned victorious. In May Ataman Dutov, a graduate of a military college who had attained the rank of lieutenant-general in the White army, captured the village of Aleksandrov Gai and had 2,000 members of the Red Army buried alive. He also executed 700 villagers. In Siberia Admiral Kolchak persecuted any and all socialists, perceived or not, in 1919 ordering that his generals destroy entire villages.

Kornilov's troops lay down their arms. (Yakov Vladimirovich Steinberg)

In September 1918 Cossack warlords committed several, uncounted atrocities, torturing and killed hundreds of people. It was reported that the victims' eyes were gouged out, their tongues cut out and many were buried alive. Specialist 'death houses' were set up where several forms of torture were practised. When White forces took towns and villages, regardless of any political affiliation therein, executions were immediately carried out. The Czech Legion fighting for the Whites were not immune. In May 1918, in Chelyabinsk, they executed every member of the local council. When they invaded Penza they executed 250 pro-Soviet Czechs.

There seemed to be little effort in bothering to hide the extremes that those involved in the Terror would go to. This is an excerpt from an interview with Felix Dzerzhinsky, published in *Novaya Zhizn* on 14 July 1918:

We stand for organized terror—this should be frankly admitted. Terror is an absolute necessity during times of revolution. Our aim is to fight against the enemies of the Soviet Government and of the new order of life. We judge quickly. In most cases only a day passes between the apprehension of the criminal and his sentence. When confronted with evidence criminals in almost every case confess; and what argument can have greater weight than a criminal's own confession.

British troops, as forces of occupation, found themselves scattered across Europe after the war. These members of the Honourable Artillery Company haul lumber in Austria.

There were widespread stories in the British press concerning the Red Terror. *The Times* of 12 September 1918 led a story with the headline, "Soviet Appeal for Massacre". According to the story the Russian press was giving out biased views of the fighting in Russia while at the same time appealing for violent action against the bourgeoisie, the entente and all other anti-Bolshevik forces. An article in the *Krasnaya Gazeta* in September 1918 stated,

> We will turn our hearts into steel which we will temper in the fire of suffering and the blood of the fighters for freedom. We will make our hearts cruel, hard and immoveable so that no mercy will enter them and that they will not quiver at the sight of a sea of enemy blood.

The correspondent of the *New York World* who had just escaped from Petrograd in September 1918 said that Zinoviev, the president of the Petrograd Soviet, had ordered the execution of 500 prisoners, not because they were counter-revolutionaries but because they were of the educated classes. He went on to explain that eradicating the educated classes had always been the Bolshevik aim but they could only do it by making their foot soldiers become so brutalized by the continuous execution of counter-revolutionaries that they would be willing to kill anyone when ordered to.

Lenin, Voroshilov (behind Lenin) and Trotsky (just to the right of Lenin, his left shoulder facing slightly left) with soldiers—the participants in the liquidation of the Kronstadt uprising—among the delegates to the Tenth Congress of the Russian Communist Party—, 21 March 1921. (Leon Leonidov)

Above left: Bolshevik justice, Hungary, 1919. (Rudolph Balogh)

Above right: White Terror, Hungary, 1919.

Below: White Terror in the Ukraine. (Острогорский М.)

There had been some representation to the Bolshevik government in Petrograd by the neutral powers in early September against the massacres taking place, including the Dutch minister representing the interests of Great Britain, Japan and Belgium and the Danish minister representing France and Siam. The Norwegian minister represented the United States and Romania and the Swiss minister Italy. It was reported that numbers of murders declined after this but that arrests of large numbers of the upper classes were still taking place.

The position of British citizens in Petrograd was worrying to the British press. The British naval attaché Captain Cromie had been murdered, for example. *The Times* correspondent reported that there had been orders in Russia not to accept any more telegrams from British subjects who were also prohibited from using certain rail routes, restrictions in force while Allied troops remained in Russia. The French and Americans had similar restrictions imposed on them but according to *The Times* correspondent it was the British who were seen as the main antagonists of the Soviet government.

The Times in July 1919 published excerpts from a document published by the Bolsheviks which stated the following:

With the aid of Russian blackguards hundreds of English capitalists are capturing one town after another, taking away our crops, slaughtering our brethren, violating our wives and sisters and robbing our homes. As they look on these English brigands the Germans who are the most insatiable of all our foes are sharpening their teeth for a raid on Petrograd.

As well as the number of deaths due to execution there had also been an outbreak of cholera in Petrograd which, along with starvation, was the cause of hundreds of deaths a day. There was not enough wood for coffins and bodies were being taken to cemeteries wrapped in newspaper where they often lay unburied for days. To combat this members of the bourgeoisie who hadn't already been arrested were forced to the cemeteries to dig graves. Some of these luminaries, once been the richest men in the city, were often arrested then released on payment of huge fines before being rearrested. One ex-mayor had been forced to dig graves on a number of occasions.

The shortage of food was being blamed on the theft of supplies by foreigners. There was no doubt that the Germans had executed peasants in the Ukraine who resisted the requisition of their grain and the Bolsheviks were now doing exactly the same, not always too easily. Peasants near Luga organized themselves and fought back. Three truckloads of dead soldiers were brought back to Petrograd by train.

While the rich were being forced to dig graves, former Tsarist officers were being arrested and sent to Kronstadt where thousands were forced to load coal onto warships while fed the barest minimum and subjected to a range of other cruelties. In Kharkov hundreds of men were taken to a yard in the Bolshevik headquarters where they were made to dig a massive pit and then shot. When the executioners tired of the killings, a man named Salinko continued, shooting dozens more on

Graves—often dug by members of the bourgeoisie— in front of the Winter Palace for victims of the revolution.

his own. Other victims were thrown into a sewer and left to drown. Many were tortured and large numbers were buried alive. In one cellar full of bodies even children numbered among the victims. In the Crimea a number of priests were shot. The Terror was later expanded to include anyone who might pose a threat to the Bolshevik Party or its policies, including former Tsarists, liberals, Mensheviks, members of the Russian Orthodox Church, foreigners, and anyone who dared to sell food or goods for profit. Peasants who refused to meet state requisition orders were labelled as *kulaks*, greedy speculators who hoarded grain and food for profit while other Russians starved. Later, industrial workers who failed to meet production quotas or dared to strike were also targeted. As the Bolsheviks expanded their definition of who constituted an enemy of the revolution, they also expanded the Cheka. A small force of just a few hundred men in early 1918 was supposed to be a temporary measure: within two years the Cheka was a large government agency employing around 200,000 people.

Although there is little doubt that there were atrocities carried out by the various White forces, there was almost no reporting of such in the British press. One article that did appear on White terror concerned Hungary. There had been claims of atrocities committed after the fall of the short-lived Soviet government in Hungary

Above: Corpses of victims of the 1918 Red Terror in Evpatoria, dumped by Bolshevists executioners in the Black Sea, but later washed ashore.

Right: Red Terror victim, Hungary, 1919. The original caption read: "The Lenin boys pose for their photograph with their victim." (Cécile Tormay)

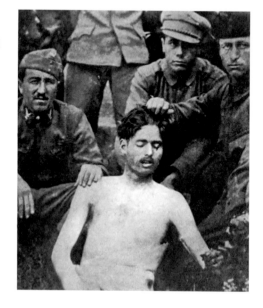

Funeral of Moisei Uritsky, Petrograd, 2 September 1918. The banner reads: "Death to the bourgeois and their helpers. Long live the Red Terror."

The Bolsheviks have just visited a Kharkiv Govcheka yard at 5, Sadova Street.

Above: People massacred by Bolsheviks on 14 January 1919 in Tartu Krediidikassa, Estonia.

Right: Polish Captain Rosinsky being tortured by Red Army soldiers, 1918.

in August 1919, claims that British officers were involved. An inquiry was launched by the secretary of state for foreign affairs and it was found that a number of Bolsheviks did suffer at the hands of the public before the new government could assert its authority and stop reprisals. A number of those involved were later prosecuted and some found guilty of murder. Admiral Trowbridge had been in the country for some time and supplied information on the killings. It was believed that nearly 400 Bolsheviks had been murdered in revenge killings and that the victims were nearly all Jews. There were further reports of White terror in Hungary in 1920 in the *Manchester Guardian* which stated that communists were still being executed but this was by the government, with a letter published in the newspaper from Bertrand Russell asking the Allies to intervene in the case of Professor Varjaz, a philosopher who was in danger of being executed.

Many area suffered from both Red and White terror. When Riga in Latvia was under the control of the Bolsheviks killings and torture were commonplace and widespread. When the fell to the Whites, the killings continued unabated. The British Commissioner in the Baltic, a Board of Trade official by the name of Lieutenant-Colonel Stephen Tallents, attempted to intervene by asking a man named Fletcher, commander of the Baltic Landwehr (Baltic Territorial Army), to stop the killings. He was told that 200 of the 4,000 prisoners had already been executed. Thirty-three men and seven women were being executed each morning. Fletcher then went on to describe the forms of torture that had been carried out by the Bolsheviks and said that the worst offenders were women.

Although the Bolsheviks well perceived the dangers from the Allies after they had defeated Germany there was no combined policy among the Allies as to the new Russian government. The Allies seemed happy to leave the Whites to battle it out, with notional support in terms of Allied matériel. There was also a peculiar view that the Bolsheviks had been supported by the Germans and that they would fade away after the German defeat. By early 1919 most Allied troops in Russia had been withdrawn apart from the British in Batum who stayed on until the autumn. By November Lloyd George suggested that relations with Russia should be normalized and in December decided to halt any further intervention in Russia and instead form a cordon sanitaire.

7. DENOUEMENT

The effects of the revolution and the civil war were strongly evident in Russia by 1922. There was widespread famine which had begun in the previous year that added to the litany of droughts, failed harvests and conflict since 1914. The numbers of those who died from starvation and disease have been widely disputed and vary in estimation from one to ten million. The most frequently given figure seems to be around five million. The reasons for the famine have also been disputed but there seems little doubt that the forced collectivization of farms and the requisition of grain and seed by the Soviet authorities were in part to blame. Peasants could not plant crops if they had no seed, and anyway there was no incentive for them to do so if the resulting crop was going to be taken from them. The economic blockade of Russia by the Allies also was a major cause of the famine. The Allies might have not been at war with the Russian government but that had little to do with their actions which in many cases were no different to what would have occurred had they been at war. There was a similar blockade on Germany for many years after the end of the war which resulted in millions of Germans going hungry; the difference being that in Germany the Allied forces of occupation were witness to the disaster on a daily basis and the British soldiers often fed the starving Germans despite government policy forbidding it.

The Labour Party in Britain published a pamphlet on famine conditions in central Europe in 1919. Agreement was reached at the Southport Conference of the Labour Party in 1919 which stated

Memorial card for Lord Settrington (Charles Henry Gordon Lennox), a lieutenant in the Irish Guards who died of his wounds in North Russia in August 1919.

Map of the famine area of Soviet Russia, 1921. (*Russian Information and Review* magazine)

"its empathic protest against the methods of starvation, especially when used against women and children, as an instrument of Government policy". The comments concerned the blockade of Central Europe, with the Labour Party calling for arrangements on an international basis to allocate commodities to countries based on their need not their ability to pay. The report discussed Russia and stated that in Moscow hospitals 80 percent of women died in childbirth as did 90 percent of newborn infants. There were terrible typhus and smallpox epidemics in the country against which the government had no means to fight. There was not even enough wood for coffins for the dead or transport to take the bodies to cemeteries. The report quoted a Russian writer who described the situation first-hand:

after a time the spectacle of misery ceases to make any appeal to sympathy. It just makes the instinct of self-preservation keener. At the sight of those who are most miserable they make provision to escape a similar fate. They see to it that they collect more foodstuffs and take care to hide it.

These Lithuanian soldiers fought for the newly independent Lithuania against the Bolsheviks.

The British government had a very good idea of the conditions in Russia. In a report from one factory, the Pulitov Works, it was stated that there had been 40,000 workers before the war but were only 7,000 left at the time of the report—1920—with the workers explaining that they were starving and existed on bread and Soviet soup. They were exhausted due to excessive overtime and not enough to eat; they could not afford what food was available. A worker explained that

> cold and hunger have taught us much. The most important thing is that we have learnt to understand why it is that we are starving. It is now becoming sufficiently clear that we are getting bread with difficulty because we don't give the peasants manufactured goods and that we can't transport the grain lying ready in the corn-bearing government [warehouses] because there is no transport to move it.

It was also obvious to the population that in a country full of forests they had no fuel to keep the factory furnaces going because they could not supply the forest workers with bread so they got no wood. It was that simple.

The 1919 harvest had been a good one in Russia but was not repeated in 1920; according to Muralov, a well-known communist agricultural expert, the only way to deal with this was to grind up old stocks of corn in Siberia and the Urals; this was based on the hopes of a good harvest in 1921. In January 1921 Lenin stated that there was a need to increase the export of grain from places such as Samara, Kazan, Saratov and Tambov. This was due to the lack of fuel that meant that it had been impossible to obtain more than half the food ordered from the Caucasus. One of the major problems was explained in relation to Siberia. Western Siberia had been unable to export grain which was causing severe problems in eastern Siberia. The division between town and country had become glaringly apparent since Soviet administration had been established in Siberia. The peasants strongly opposed the new administration and refused to supply the urban areas with grain.

Although the British government continued to enforce a blockade of much of Central Europe—which in turn exacerbated the dire problems facing Russian— many members of the British public were sympathetic to the plight of the Russians as they were to the Germans. Appeals for help came from British workers such as Harry Pollitt, a communist who visited Russia in 1921. Pollitt was a member of the 'Hands off Russia' campaign that was strongly opposed to Allied intervention in the Russian civil war. His article, entitled 'A Cry from Russia', published in the Boilermakers & Iron and Steel Shipbuilders Union journal, attracted much attention, contesting the government view that the Russian famine had been caused by the Bolsheviks, something almost gleefully expounded by the British press. According to Pollitt, had the Bolsheviks had not been in power the fate of the Russian people would have been

Above: Two small coffins being carried on stretchers to the cemetery in the Volga famine district, 1921. (Library of Congress)

Right: Entrepreneurial cannibals selling heads and body parts at an impromptu market, Samara province, Volga region, Russia, 1921. (Eric Baschet)

Left: A starving 7-year-old girl who has a swollen stomach due to prolonged starvation, and because she has eaten grass, in the village of Sojekjejevo, Buguruslan, 1921. (Fridtjof Nansen)

Below: Peasants of the Bouzuluk district and the remains of the humans they have eaten, 1921. (Eric Baschet)

even worse. He claimed that there was no case where there was unequal distribution of food in the country and that workers, peasants and soldiers all widely supported revolution. He claimed that Allied support for the Whites in the civil war had led to an economic meltdown due to the destruction of the transport system and the need for skilled men to fight in the Red Army. Pollitt did admit however that the severe drought was also partly to blame.

He went on to say that Russia was surrounded by hostile states such as Finland, Estonia, Latvia, Poland and Romania, all supported by Britain and France, and ready to bring down the revolution.

The Times of course saw thing slightly differently, suggesting that "the Bolsheviks had defied Western Governments while they wrecked Russia and having failed to overthrow the European economic system by a frontal attack were now trying to turn its flank", and seeing it as a victory for the Bolsheviks if they could induce western governments to contribute to the maintenance of Russia. The paper went on to describe Russia as "tottering on the brink of collapse amid the ruin it had created itself". Bolshevism and international finance—capitalism—were supposedly sworn enemies but the Russian pleas for help were based on humanitarian issues. Yet perversely, the friendly overtures being made by Russia did not however mean that they had abandoned their aim of destroying capitalism. *The Times* was therefore cynical of both sides, based on the reality of the relationship between Russia and the West at the time.

Meanwhile, while the politicians of Europe schemed, in Russia the situation was getting worse. The Swedish Red Cross based in Samara was distributing 19,000 meals a day to the starving Russian population but was desperately appealing for 40,000 a day. The leader of the Swedish mission, M. Elkstrand, was to describe the situation in graphic terms: that there were cases of raging madness everywhere with even cases of cannibalism where children and the sick were being murdered and their bodies eaten. The Swedish organization was aided by the Soviet government and had exchanged 5,700 tons of Swedish salt herrings for the same weight of wheat, something the Soviets made much mileage out of; but it could not mask the fact, highlighted by the Swedes, of the utter indifference of the Soviet government which continued to maintain an army of a million men and several million government employees who absorbed all the resources of the country while allowing the rest of the population to starve. Such views were at variance with those of Harry Pollit who claimed that everyone in Russia was getting an equal share. In reality the conflicting views espoused by the various sides were used primarily for political purposes. It suited the West to suggest that the Bolsheviks were responsible for the famine in its entirety, that the Soviets were doing nothing to alleviate the starvation. In fact, it was mooted that the Soviets were using the famine as a useful tool to control the masses.

Above: More corpses in the Russian famine, these at Buzuluk, 1921. (Fridtjof Nansen)

Left: Starving and dirty children, plagued by lice, are having their hair cut before bathing in a railroad carriage at the station in Samara (Kujbysev). (Fridtjof Nansen)

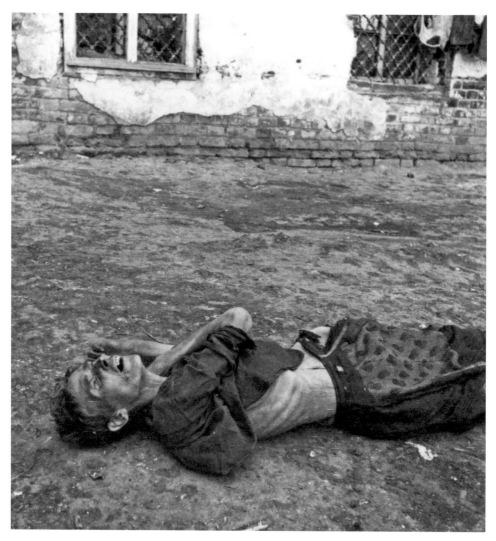

A Saratov famine victim. (Fridtjof Nansen)

Dr Fridtjof Nansen, High Commissioner for the International Committee for Russian Relief (ICRR)—set up by the International Committee of the Red Cross and the League of Red Cross Societies—claimed there were provinces in Russia where ten to fifteen million people would not live through the winter of 1921/22 without help. He presented slideshows to prove this and went on to argue that, quite apart from the humanitarian view, there was also a serious economic threat to Europe unless the situation was brought under control. Europe could not afford to let one of the greatest granaries in the world become a depopulated desert. He claimed that he had

Piles of corpses of famine victims. (Fridtjof Nansen)

the agreement of the Soviet government that every ounce of food that was donated would be used where it was needed, that the regeneration of the Russian economy was necessary to regenerate the economy of Europe. The claims that the Soviet government was not helping were false, he claimed: they were doing all they could but were themselves weak because of the dire situation that they had inherited.

An endless stream of senior diplomats was being sent to Russia to see for themselves what the situation was. Sir Benjamin Robertson, formerly Chief Commissioner of the Central Province of India, arrived back in London in February 1922 from Russia. He had wide experience of famine in India and had gone to Russia at the request of Lord Emmet's Committee of the Russian Relief Fund. Sir Benjamin was struck by the similarity of the rural conditions in Russia to those in India. The village community was very similar. In India it had been landless labourers and small-scale peasant farmers that needed famine relief; in Russia it was the entire population.

The glaring reason, as mentioned, was that there was no grain left in the country primarily because it had all been requisitioned. In one village he was told by the chairman of the executive committee that out of 400 horses the village once boasted, only thirty-two were left and only ten of those were fit to work. A herd of cows once numbering 300 was now down to less than forty. The requisition of grain in 1919 had been moderate but in 1920 had been all-encompassing. Requisition had been abandoned in 1921 because there was nothing left to take. Some seed had been provided by the government in 1921 but not enough to raise a decent crop. The chairman was responsible for 7,000 people over ten villages. In December 1921 there had been twelve deaths of children from starvation and eight from illness. Thirty-five adults had died from starvation and twenty-three from sickness. Many were buried in mass graves. Even the wealthier suffered: where they normally had on average twelve horses and eight cows, most had only one of each left. Many poorer families had no grain at all.

In India the problem of famine was solved by buying food through private trade. This had initially been banned in Russia but was later permitted—a case of too little too late—there was nothing to buy and even had there been, the transport system had collapsed. Sir Benjamin had first-hand experience of this. When he tried to travel to Samara the locomotive broke down with a subsequent delay of twenty-five days. He then managed to take a train to Moscow; it was the first train for three weeks as the line had been blocked by snow. Some twenty-five people perished on the train from typhus, cold and starvation while it was held up. Sir Benjamin said that conditions were the worst he had ever seen, far worse than anything he had experienced in India.

Many children were abandoned by their starving parents and left to die. The government had opened several children's home for abandoned children but he witnessed many such children begging for bread around the homes.

One home that Sir Benjamin inspected in Samara contained around 800 children, eighty of whom had been collected that day, five of them he described as dying. In Buzuluk he saw a receiving home that was supposed to hold sixty children but in fact held four hundred. There was little more than standing room and their rations consisted of a small slice of rye bread a day. After ten days in a receiving home, the children were then transferred to a quarantine home where they were washed and disinfected. They were then divided into sick and healthy. The healthy were sent to permanent homes when places became available where they also received some education. The sick either went to hospital or stayed in the quarantine home. It did seem that the government was doing its best for the children within its limited means.

In Samara there were two receiving homes, two quarantine homes and seventy-four permanent homes containing thousands of children. Twenty train loads of children each carrying 400 to 600 had already been evacuated. Sir Benjamin said that Samara wasn't as bad as Buzuluk. He went on to say that it was only children who were being cared for by foreign aid. Adults had until this time been left to starve

A child market in Russia where peasants sold their children as servants in exchange for food.

unless they were helped by the Soviet government. The Americans had by now realized how bad the situation was and were beginning to send maize to feed the adults. Sir Benjamin then urged the British government to do the same. In one particular region where British aid workers were operational, over a million adults were starving. Sir Benjamin also visited Moscow where he described the situation as serious. The population was listless and suffering from gloom. On 1 December 1921 a pound of black bread cost 4,000 roubles; by 31 January 1922 it cost 28,000 roubles. A one rouble note at this time had a statement printed on the back saying that it was the equivalent of 10,000 roubles. By the end of January the rouble was 1,900,000 to the British pound, a rate of inflation similar to what was shortly to occur in Germany.

The situation continued to worsen and in May a letter sent from Novorossick on the Black Sea said that the writer had witnessed scenes of horror in the harbour where people were dying of hunger and fever but it was worse in the interior. In the northern part of Taurida, out of a population of 1,288,000, nearly a million were without food and all local resources were totally exhausted.

Cases of cannibalism were common. In Rostov, which had not at this time been declared a hunger zone, a man had been arrested for killing and eating his wife. In Tsarirtsyn the death rate for April 1922 was 56 percent of the population. People were eating bark off the trees, straw and weeds.

It was quite clear that the economic policy in Russia was failing apart as a result of the famine. Trusts and cooperative concerns that were in some ways a move toward

A 1919 1,000-rouble note when inflation in Russia almost matched Germany's hyperinflation.

The Orthodox Church was a traditional enemy of the Soviets.

privatization were as good as bankrupt. Fuel was being diverted from factories to keep the railways running so that food could be distributed. According to a report in *The Times* in early June,

> it is only food supplies from abroad and the confiscation of the wealth of the church that is keeping Russia from economic collapse. The new economic policy has in fact done little more than resulted in the enrichment of small numbers of officials who would like to see pre-revolutionary conditions return.

The extremists however were using the situation to reinforce their claims that the Genoa Conference, which attempted to introduce trade between Russia and the West, was a waste of time and that no good could ever come of attempting this. Perhaps more worrying for Europe were attempts by Germany to become Russia's sole trading partner in Europe. This seemed a worthwhile strategy for Russia as it would strengthen the position of the Soviet government and form a Russian–German front against the Allies. The Genoa Conference had not been seen as a success in Britain either as it had done little to remedy unemployment in Britain. Russia had by choice ceased to be a factor in the productive activities of the world and the rest of Europe was dominated by chaotic currencies that made trade a hazardous occupation.

The problem for Britain and the rest of Europe—and the world, for that matter—was that without trade they could ill-afford to keep pouring money and aid into Russia to help the country get back to some sort of stability.*

By June 1922 the western press was speculating on Lenin's health and a likely successor. *The Times* believed that the vacuum created by Lenin's leave of

Stalin.

absence would lead to a power struggle between Trotsky, Techitherin and Krassin, Trotsky being the most militant of the three (many felt he would embark on military action against neighbouring states). Strangely Stalin wasn't mentioned.

It was clear that Lenin saw Trotsky as his successor but Stalin had other ideas, promoting himself as a favourite of Lenin. Of course Lenin was ill—some believed due to the bullets still lodged in his body from the 1918 assassination attempt—and he did retire from public life for a period during which time Stalin cemented over Trotsky his claim to the crown.

Although the civil war was seen to be over by this time, there were still a number of groups operating against the Soviet government, known as Green Partisans. They would often arrive in towns and villages and court martial the local communist authorities. In areas where foreign aid had been distributed the partisans would often

---

* In 1920 Italy had bought and paid for a large amount of goods from Azerbaijan. Before the goods could be delivered the Azerbaijani government was overthrown, and a new Bolshevik government took over and confiscated the Italian goods. A year later the same goods that the Italians had paid for were dispatched to Milan where they were stored on behalf of the Soviet government who began selling them off—under the noses of the Italians.

lynch local officials when it was found that they had taken aid for themselves before distributing it to the people. Partisans were generally deserters from the Red Army, peasants who had lost their land and others who had lost everything to the Soviets. In many cases they were led by former Tsarist officers or officials. In the British press they were dubbed the Robin Hoods of Russia as they often redistributed goods from Soviets stores to the people. They also took the clothes from those they hanged as the only half-reasonably dressed people in Russia were the Soviets.

When Lenin returned from his hiatus he tried to put a brake on Stalin's power grab. He believed that he was becoming too powerful and wanted him removed. However the Politburo decided against it and Stalin retained his position. After Lenin's death on 21 January 1924, Trotsky was still calling for a world revolutionary movement but the more practical members of the Politburo realized that this was doomed to failure. Trotsky was removed from his position as commissar of war in 1925. Stalin was meanwhile becoming more and more powerful and despite some of Lenin's lieutenants taking Trotsky's side, it was Stalin who continued to dominate with support of the right-wing members of the Politburo.[*]

Joseph Vissarionovich Stalin became General Secretary of the Communist Party of the Soviet Union on 3 April 1922 and ruled with an iron fist for three decades until his death on 16 October 1952. The Red and White terrors of the civil war years were to pale into insignificance when compared to The Great Terror of the Stalinist regime where between nine and 50 million perished

The civil war in art, Grekov Mitrofan Borisovich's 1934 impression.

---

[*] Trotsky was forced into exile in 1928, and assassinated on Stalin's orders in Mexico City in 1940.

BIBLIOGRAPHY

Buchanan, G., *My Mission to Russia*, Cassell, London 1923

_____, *My Mission to Russia*, Vol 2, Cassell, London 1923

Carr, E. H., *The Russian Revolution from Lenin to Stalin 1917–29*, Macmillan, London 1979

Chambers, R., *The Last Englishman: The Double Life of Arthur Ransome*, Faber & Faber, London 2009

Figes, O., *A People's Tragedy, The Russian Revolution 1891–1924*, Bodley Head, London 2014

Foglesong, D., *America's Secret War Against Bolshevism*, University of North Carolina Press, Chapel Hill 1995

Harcave, S., *First Blood: The Russian Revolution of 1905*, Bodley Head, London 1964

Hastings, S., *The Secret Lives of Somerset Maugham*, Murray, London 2010

Luxemburg, R., *The Russian Revolution and Leninism or Marxism?*, Ann Arbor Paperbacks, Michigan 1961

Maugham, W. S., *Ashenden: Or the British Agent*, Heinemann, London 1956

Milton, G., *Russian Roulette*, Sceptre, London 2013

Reilly, S., *Adventures of a British Master Spy: The Memoirs of Sidney Reilly*, Biteback Publishing, London 2014

Silverlight, J. *The Victors' Dilemma: Allied Intervention in the Russian Civil War*, Barrie & Jenkins Ltd., London 1970

Index

Michael Foley spent most of his working life as a teacher in east London. Fifteen years ago, at the age of 45, he gave up teaching to become a full-time carer for his disabled grandson, which is when he began to write seriously. Since then he has had more than thirty books published, mainly local and military titles as well as three novels as ebooks. He has written numerous magazine articles, short stories and a weekly newspaper column for West Ham United supporters.

He lives in Romford with his wife, grandson and three dogs.

OTHER HISTORY OF TERROR TITLES

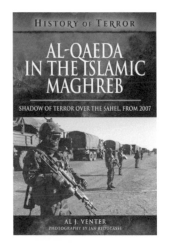

HISTORY of TERROR
AL-QAEDA IN THE ISLAMIC MAGHREB
SHADOW OF TERROR OVER THE SAHEL, FROM 2007

AL J. VENTER
PHOTOGRAPHY BY JAN REDUCASSE

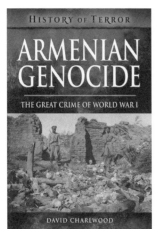

HISTORY of TERROR
ARMENIAN GENOCIDE
THE GREAT CRIME OF WORLD WAR I

DAVID CHARLWOOD

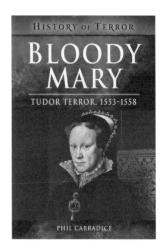

HISTORY of TERROR
BLOODY MARY
TUDOR TERROR, 1553–1558

PHIL CARRADICE

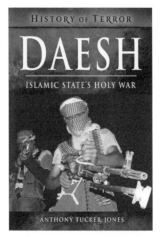

HISTORY of TERROR
DAESH
ISLAMIC STATE'S HOLY WAR

ANTHONY TUCKER-JONES

HISTORY of TERROR
SS EINSATZGRUPPEN
NAZI DEATH SQUADS, 1939–1945

GERRY VAN TONDER

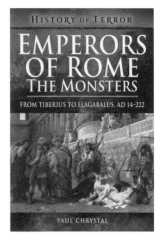

HISTORY of TERROR
EMPERORS OF ROME
THE MONSTERS
FROM TIBERIUS TO ELAGABALUS, AD 14–222

PAUL CHRYSTAL

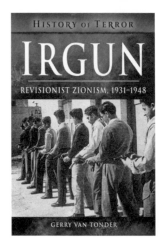

HISTORY of TERROR
IRGUN
REVISIONIST ZIONISM, 1931–1948

GERRY VAN TONDER

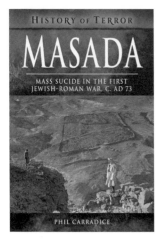

HISTORY of TERROR
MASADA
MASS SUCIDE IN THE FIRST JEWISH-ROMAN WAR, C. AD 73

PHIL CARRADICE

HISTORY of TERROR
NIGHT OF THE LONG KNIVES
HITLER'S EXCISION OF ROHM'S SA BROWNSHIRTS, 30 JUNE–2 JULY 1934

PHIL CARRADICE

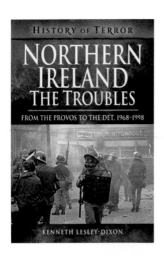

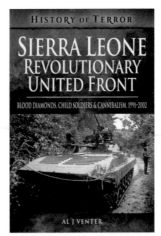

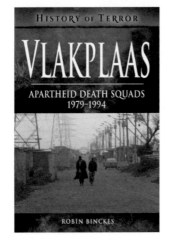

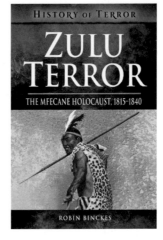